THE PURSUIT OF CITIZENSHIP

BRUCE A. WEITZ

THE PURSUIT OF CITIZENSHIP

PAST, PRESENT, PROMISE

credo
house publishers

Published in the United States of America by Credo House Publishers,
a division of Credo Communications, LLC, Grand Rapids, Michigan
credohousepublishers.com

Unless otherwise indicated, all Scripture is taken from the New American Standard Bible®, copyright © 1960, 1971, 1977, 1995, 2020 by The Lockman Foundation. All rights reserved.

ISBN: 978-1-62586-304-1

Cover and interior design by Frank Gutbrod
Editing by Donna Huisjen

Printed in the United States of America
First edition

With fondness to Al and Mary Weitz, Dad and Mom

PROLOGUE

This book developed through a burden for people, and for our nation. I am not ashamed to admit that the writing was accompanied by prayer and tears. My desire for us as American citizens and would-be Americans is that our stories be told. So, I tell them. I hope my words can be a help and encouragement to those who are in a "pursuit of citizenship." I long for a better America and a recognition that this country is worthy of our citizenship—despite all its faults. More important than that, though, is that we as Christians, because of Christ's death and resurrection, have the privilege to live our time here as a "citizen of heaven," a status of which we are not in ourselves worthy.

CONTENTS

Citizenship:
Condition of being a citizen.
Duties, rights, and privileges of a citizen.[1]

PART 1

PAST AND PRESENT

CHAPTER 1

MY ANCESTORS

Being a citizen is something that should never be taken for granted. Citizenship goes far beyond having a basic right to vote, as important as that right is. The foundation of citizenship that we have in the United States of America is unique, distinct, and special. Although other nations have aspects of what we have, our rights and privileges have never been duplicated to the degree that we enjoy them with our Constitution and Bill of Rights. It is beneficial to ask ourselves not only, "What kind of citizen am I?" but also, "What kind of country do I want to be a citizen of?"

My reflections about citizenship have led me to include a chronicle of my family history, as far as I understand it; some on my own life history and views; where we are at as a nation; and the idea of ultimate citizenship.

My family history is one of immigrants becoming citizens who contributed to the growth of our nation. I am in the line of what is now seven generations of the Weitz family from Dubuque, Iowa. My great-great-grandfather was a pioneer resident of Dubuque. Peter Weitz was born in Jugesheim, Hesse-Darmst, Germany in 1805 and arrived in America on July 4, 1854, with his family (their arrival in Dubuque would have been in 1855).

At the time his son, my great-grandfather, was seven. Peter Weitz was a farmer/gardener, but apparently farming didn't work out for him when he got to America, so he hired on as a gardener. He was listed on the 1890 census as a retired farmer.

The name Weitz has its origin in the occupational name for wheat grower or dealer. My great-grandfather was also named Peter. Peter Eduard would grow up and marry Sibilla Fosselman; he was a painter in a blacksmith shop owned by George Bock. The younger Peter painted the molded parts for wagons and later for automobiles. Peter moved on in his career to work for A. A. Cooper Wagon and Buggy Company. He started out as a painter, then made parts, and finally became a foreman.

In 1875 the wagon company had ninety employees and produced three thousand wagons annually, and in 1877 the employees worked twelve-hour days. "In 1897 the company employed 300 men who worked thirteen to fourteen hour days to keep up with demand. In 1910 the company's six hundred workers [together] took home an annual payroll of a quarter of a million dollars. 'Old Reliable' as the Cooper wagons were known, were praised for their dependability. Cooper learned from his apprenticeship of the superiority of naturally seasoned over kiln-dried woods and required that all wood used in his wagons be seasoned up to seven years."[2] It was said that Cooper wagons were sold in every civilized nation in the world.

"Among the early trades, blacksmithing deserves special attention. Blacksmiths shoed horses, forged iron, and fashioned all sorts of tools and mechanisms. They occupied a unique position as the pioneer community's most versatile and 'most indispensable mechanic.' The blacksmith shop, moreover, operate[d] as a gathering place to socialize. The 1850 census listed nine blacksmith establishments, outnumbering any other enterprise and employing two to six workers each. Those who worked in blacksmithing earned average monthly wages of $22.00."[3]

Employees of the George Bock Wagon and Blacksmith Shop at 22nd and Clay Streets take a break on a sunny day in 1913. From the left are Bill Hank; George Bock, Sr.; Pete Weitz; Emil Bock; and George Bock, Jr. (Courtesy of Ruth Heitzman, daughter of Emil Bock). (Dubuque, the Birthplace of Iowa)

It should be noted that I am indebted to my brother Jerry for his countless hours of research into our family genealogy. Many families have a member willing to spend time and money to research family history. The family tree can be fascinating but is sometimes avoided due to the risks of finding a member with a sordid past, a notorious criminal, or a past that reveals a shrub rather than a family tree (even though we are all members of the massive family tree of the human race). Jerry became interested in our heritage because at one point he heard relatives discussing our family background. He became curious and took it on for himself to research the lineage. It was a painstaking process involving library (looking through microfiche), courthouse, cemetery, and neighborhood trips. He did most of this without the use of a computer and the internet, as this type of information wasn't on the internet at that time.

One aspect of the lives of my ancestors and the family I grew up in was our religious background. We had strong ties to Catholicism. As one who is no longer Catholic, I now see this as an aspect of our history I am intrigued by, not just because of my roots but because of my gratitude today for something greater. This thankfulness goes deeper than the roots of blood ties and religious tradition. The faith I now have provides something better than that in which I was raised. More on this later.

Peter E. and Sibilla would end up having seven children, the youngest of whom, Alois Otto (how is that for a German name?), was my grandfather. Alois married Nellie Gloden and became a grocer. He and his brother Peter established two Weitz Bros. grocery stores. Hard times came, the Great Depression hit, and Peter died in 1932. One store was sold, and the other became a tavern. Alois and Nellie lived next door to the tavern on East 22nd Street in Dubuque. In their small duplex they would raise six children. The second to the youngest—as I would be—Aloysius (known as Al), was my father.

There seems to be some mystery to my dad's name. His birth certificate lists him as Alois Lawrence. In his father's obituary he is Aloise Weitz Jr., and in his mother's obituary, Alois Weitz. He went by Aloysius or Al and listed his name as Aloysius Lawrence Weitz on his marriage certificate. Dad never told any of us kids about his name or if he had ever had it legally changed. Regardless, after the death of his parents Al would marry and (for a time) go on to live in the duplex he'd been raised in. The couple would wisely move, due to my mother's push to find something more suitable, as they wasted no time in having three more children. Eventually they had ten children within ten years, with one child—a girl—being stillborn. The house we nine kids were raised in is still in the family and is owned by one of my brothers.

Growing up in a large family meant that our parents had to be creative. In our kitchen was a cafeteria style dispenser that held five gallons of milk. We had benches down the sides of the kitchen table instead of chairs. For the boys' bedroom my parents acquired single hospital beds that were stacked to make bunk beds. That made it a bit easier to accommodate eight boys in one room. We got to pick what color we wanted our bed to be painted.

This setup could cause problems—if the brother getting into the upper bunk wasn't careful, the bed could topple (as the head and foot had rounded corners). That happened one night to me, although I didn't realize it since I was asleep! When I woke up the next morning with a chipped front tooth, we figured that this mishap had taken place. There are always funny stories to share in a large family—although I would have preferred to eliminate the detail of the chipped tooth!

Reflecting back, what were the reasons my ancestors left Germany? What was going on in the years leading up to 1854? What could have been some of the issues that caused them to be willing to leave behind their livelihoods and families and start anew in a different country?

CHAPTER 2

IMMIGRATION

The decision to emigrate can result from a variety of reasons. These are called the push/pull factors of immigration. The "push" can be the consequence of any number of problems in a person's homeland, while the "pull" is often the benefits of life in a new country. In the 1850s nearly one million Germans came to America; in 1854 alone there were 215,000 Germans who would arrive in this country.[4]

The first of the "push" factors was undoubtedly the failed revolution of 1848 that had attempted to establish democracy. During this period there were many uprisings all over Europe. In February 1848 revolution took place in Paris, and four weeks later, in the spring of 1848, conditions were right for the same to occur in Germany. The protests were against monarchial absolutism and particularism.[5] Contributing conditions were population growth and shifts.

The population in Germany almost doubled in the century between 1740 and 1840, and that growth meant that the farm economy couldn't meet the needs of the increased population, especially during times of poor harvest. Many would end up destitute. The shift of people from rural to urban areas also led to many labor shortages. With those conditions there are always people readily available to start a revolution, such as in Victor Hugo's masterpiece novel *Les Misérables*.[6]

In Germany, those leading the cause were made up of the growing middle class, many of them well educated, who were set "against the privilege of birth of the nobility."[7] "And as a revolution is not just rebellion against oppressive rule, but always bound to hope and the belief in a better future . . . they proclaimed and pursued two main aims; personal liberty and national unity."[8]

The Revolution of 1848 was deemed a failure for a variety of reasons. The Prussian king Frederick William IV refused the crown, and the government had trained military superiority over people on the barricades. The revolutionaries also had differences and division over aims and tactics and were "trying to tackle too much on too many fronts."[9]

Although the revolution failed, it wasn't considered a complete failure because "after 1850 almost all German states, even Prussia, had at least some kind of constitution and parliament. Most important of all: the revolution had again put the problem of the German Nation-State on the agenda."[10]

A German nation-state was brought about less than twenty-five years later. This was due not to revolution "from below" but to political outcomes "from above." This involved Prussia's victory over Austria, culminating a kind of civil war in 1866. There had been ongoing rivalry between the two regions up to that point.[11] Thus, many people at this time would have the motivation they needed to move from Germany, my ancestors among them.

While the factors of civil war, societal struggle, and labor and food issues caused migration, there was also religious opposition to prompt it. Religious oppression, which was to become a greater issue under Otto von Bismarck, the first chancellor and

Prime Minister of the German Empire (which is what it became in 1871), incited a fight against the Catholic Church. The political wing of the Catholic minority, the Centre Party, was opposed to helping strengthen Bismark's alliance with National-Liberals. The conflict became known as the Kulturkampf (culture struggle) in the 1870s.

Bismarck abolished many rights and privileges of the Catholic Church, leading to the "expulsion of the Jesuits from the Reicht, to establish state control over education but also over the appointment of clergy . . . along with authorizing the seizure of church property and the expulsion and even imprisonment of some members of the church."[12]

It is said that Bismarck "had underestimated the stubborn, passive resistance of the German Catholics, and in the end the two sides were locked in a stalemate. After the death of the militant Pope Pius IX in 1878 the struggle was slowly wound up in a number of compromises."[13]

I find the above quote interesting because I have seen firsthand the stubborn pride of the German Catholic, along with my own often self-righteous and equally obstinate pride. It is also of interest because of a great aunt of mine who became a nun. Emily Gloden, an aunt on my grandmother's side, would be named Sister Mary Cortona Gloden—the first woman to receive a degree from Columbia (now Loras College, the oldest college in Iowa, founded in 1839). She became a teacher and wrote a history titled *The Sisters of the Holy Cross of Strasbourg*.

When Sister Mary wrote the history, she needed to know the German language, which was taught in the schools at the time, but she also included information about Kulturkampf. The book was finished by others because she died of cardiac failure following an operation for a fibroid tumor of the uterus in 1926 at age 43. If a Catholic family includes a priest or a nun, this is an indication of how devout and entrenched they are in that faith.

Sister Mary Cortona Gloden. Weitz family album, estimated date 1920.

What started in the 1770s and continued for a time thereafter is called "chain migration." We in the United States are facing the consequences of chain migration now, albeit originating from a different part of the world, as many people make the trek across our borders. In the current instance there is also the issue of legality. Beyond chain migration, what we are seeing today is called mass migration—or, as some would call it, an invasion.

When many of the immigrants in the 1800s made their way to the US and became established here, they wrote letters to family and friends back home describing the opportunities they now had in America, and those letters circulated in German newspapers and books. This was probably true with regard to my great-great-grandmother, as she had either a brother or another close relative who immigrated and settled at Dubuque in 1852. Also, during this time emigration restrictions were eased. Steam ships replaced sailing ships, and the transatlantic journey became more accessible and tolerable. Sailing across the ocean in the 1850s took forty to ninety days and was dangerous due to potential shipwrecks, fires, and diseases.[14]

From the seventeenth century up to 1890, individuals of German ethnic origin outnumbered immigrants from any other country to America. "Today approximately 58 million Americans claim German ancestry. They are most numerous in California, followed by Pennsylvania, Ohio, Illinois, and Texas. The most dense German American populations are in the "German belt"— Wisconsin, Minnesota, North Dakota, South Dakota, Nebraska, and Iowa."[15] Iowa lists one of its largest ancestor groups as being German at 35.7 percent. Their settling in these states makes sense since many were farmers.

It is also important to note that during this time many territories were becoming states. I am reminded of one of my wife's favorite books, *Song of Years* by Bess Streeter Aldrich.[16] It recounts the lives of people who settled in Iowa in 1854 in the towns of Sturgis Falls and Prairie Rapids (now known as Cedar Falls and Waterloo). In this book Dubuque is also mentioned frequently, as trips had to be made back and forth for supplies. The book provides a sense of what life was like in those years; it gives account of settling the land, developing farms and communities, and developing relationships and romances.

Although my father's ancestors were most likely farmers, my mother's definitely were so. That side of my family immigrated from Czechoslovakia in 1861, landing in America on June 24, having sailed on the Oldenburg Bark *J. Ahlers*. The *J. Ahlers* sailed from Bremen, Germany, to Baltimore, Maryland, and carried a manifest of the passengers on board. Of the 326 passengers, three have the surname Bohowic. Johann was one of them, but his name was misspelled; it should have been Rohovic (which was later changed to Rohowetz). Johann, at the age of 27, would settle in Wisconsin and become my great-great-grandfather.

On my father's side of the family we haven't been able to find information about the ship Peter and Anna took to America. It should be noted that Anna was Peter's second wife. Peter and his first wife, Catharina, had been married for ten years and had two children. A couple of other children had died, as had Catharina while giving birth. Seven months later Peter married Anna.

No doubt those hardships would contribute to the notion of a new life elsewhere. Since Anna had a connection to a relative in Dubuque, that became the destination. It is possible that they landed in New Orleans on July 4, 1854, as many ships ported there because of the cotton industry. They would have made their way up the Mississippi, as passage by steamboat was relatively cheap, and arrived in Dubuque in 1855.

While many people learned about the United States from their family members, others came across promotional materials for parts of the country. One such booklet by Nathan H. Parker was titled *Iowa as It Is in 1855; A Gazetteer for Citizens and a Hand-book for Immigrants*. The book's lengthy subtitle was "Embracing a Full Description of the State of Iowa: Her agricultural, mineralogical, and geological character: Her water courses, Timberlands, soil and climate; Railroad lines built and projected, number of churches and schools in each County; Population and Business Statistics of the Most Important Cities and Towns."

The introduction to this book lists Native Americans as a primary concern in terms of settling the land. Parker was all about assuring his readers that the Native Americans had been dealt with and were not to be a threat. He dramatically wrote, "Civilization required his departure; the destiny of his outcast race bade him fly from before the coming white man's face, and take another step toward that extinction which yawns before the savage tribe. He raised his voice, once more, in cries of anguish, then joined the mighty Ishmaelitish host, and taking up the line of march, he pressed his farewell footprint on his native soil, and left behind him on the spreading plains, the last Indian trail of Iowa."[17] "Ishmael" in that paragraph refers to the son (by Hagar) of the biblical Abraham—the son who was driven into the wilderness by Sarah. (Genesis 21:9–21).

This would have been the prevailing attitude of the time, although it's difficult for us today to comprehend it. Native

Americas were often viewed as "savages with tomahawk and a scalping knife, with piercing warwhoops"—some, of course, were not only viewed that way but actually were that way.[18] The settlers saw themselves as bringing civilization and freedom from the "darkness of the Indian ages."

Parker offered a fascinating rundown of statistics regarding Iowa's residents: "The population of the Territory in 1836, was 10,531; in 1840, it was 43,017; in 1850, 192,214. The census, as returned by the Secretary of State, taken in the spring of 1854, is as follows: Males, 170,302; females, 154,900; total population, 325,202. Voters, 59,984; militia, 50,284; aliens, 10,373; colored males, 258; colored females, 222; blind, 27; deaf and dumb, 28; insane, 47; idiots [spelled "idots" in the Parker text].[19]

The 1850 census was the first to include information about each individual in a household. Again, this was a reflection of the time. It's a good thing that "idiots" are not specified in the current census—there could be too many to count! That term now is rightfully considered derogatory and offensive, though at the time the reference was to individuals defined from birth as "natural fools," whom we would now see as persons born with limited mental capacity.

Of interest in this gazetteer are the descriptions from various Iowa newspapers giving account of the streams of immigrants making their way into Iowa. (It is important to note that although the term immigrant is used during this time, they were also called pioneers and settlers, which is no longer an option for immigrants). The *Dubuque Tribune* says, "Daily—yes, hourly—immigrants are arriving in this and neighboring counties from Ohio, Kentucky, Indiana, and Illinois. All are in raptures at the lovely sights which here greet their gaze; and they with one accord yield the palm to Western Iowa for lovely prairies, beautiful groves of timberland meandering streams of water."[20]

The editor of the *Keokuk Dispatch* expressed the situation this way: "No one can travel up and down the Mississippi without being astonished at the immigration constantly pouring into Iowa from all parts of the country; especially from Indiana and Ohio."[21] Parker quotes William Barrows, Esq., from *Letters on the West*, who stated, "Probably no state in the Union has ever been settled with greater rapidity, or in so short a period of time gained greater renown than Iowa."[22]

Parker, writing in 1855, predicted that Iowa's population would reach a million people by 1860. That didn't happen, due to the Financial Panic of 1857 and failing banks and railroads caused by over-speculation with railroad and real estate. The population of Iowa in 1860 was actually 674,913.[23]

The call for more settlers went out from other newspaper editors as well. The *Keokuk Whig* invited glowingly, "Therefore, we repeat, let them come—old and young, men and women, boys and girls, with or without 'plunder.' Let them flee from their tax-ridden and miserably governed Egypts in Ohio and Pennsylvania, to the Land of Promise, flowing with something better than milk and honey, and possessing capabilities such as they have hardly dreamed of. Here they shall find welcome homes; and, while they speedily help themselves to attain better fortunes, they shall also have a hand in the proud labor of building up the mighty Empire of the Mississippi Valley."[24] Descriptions relating to the number of people coming in were "throng of immigrants," "pouring in," "endless procession," and "a mighty army of invasion."[25]

Parker portrayed Dubuque as follows: "11 churches, 1 female seminary, 1 college, 5 select and common schools, 24 lawyers, and

14 physicians. The city of Dubuque, one of the largest and most densely populated in the State, is handsomely situated upon a natural terrace. The streets run parallel to each other, and owing to the peculiar soil at this location, are never muddy. The city is more compactly built, and contains greater proportion of fine buildings than any other in the State. Among these the Catholic Cathedral, courthouse, and hotels stand prominent. The city is bounded on the West by a range of high cliffs, from which the prospect of the city and county is entrancingly beautiful."[26]

From Dubuque and Its Neighborhood, *from an old catalog compiled by Harger and Blish.*

CHAPTER 3

IMMIGRATION TO DUBUQUE

Those with the urge to immigrate, or to migrate within the country for whatever reason (i.e., land, opportunity, a better life, to escape political or religious persecution, economic hardship, etc.) would go on to contribute greatly wherever they settled, and Dubuque immigrants would be no exception. Many would apply for citizenship and naturalization and were no doubt hard-working contributors to their communities. The process for attaining citizenship, thankfully, has changed to be less discriminatory and prejudiced than it used to be (citizenship was at one time restricted to "free white persons"). The first naturalization law was enacted in 1790, and it wasn't until 1952 that an act was passed that eliminated race as a bar to immigration or citizenship.[27]

Naturalization was a two-step process that required a minimum of five years. The immigrant had to reside in the United States for two years before filing a "declaration of intention" to pursue citizenship. After an additional three years, people could petition for naturalization. "Citizenship was granted to those who were able to prove to the court's satisfaction that they were of good moral character and who took the oath of allegiance to the Constitution."[28]

Would it behoove us to require something similar today in order for an individual to remain a citizen in good standing? That would require citizens to know something about our nation's founding and the Constitution. Today, to become a citizen without the process of immigration and naturalization, a person just has to be born here.

Being so far removed from those early generations of immigrants, it is difficult for us to imagine the sense of pride and thankfulness they would have experienced in being called an American. Parenthetically, it is quite possible that many of those immigrants in the mid-nineteenth century wondered if they'd made the right choice, given that so shortly after their arrival the American Civil War was underway.

What was their understanding of patriotism in terms of their new homeland? What was life like for those early settlers in Dubuque? What I know to have been true for my ancestors was very likely the case for many others. They tended to live among those adhering to the same religion, ethnic background, and language as themselves, to be surrounded not only by family and relatives but by a familiar community they could rely on. These newcomers would go on to establish clubs and societies, very often linked to a certain parish or diocese.

The East 22nd Street area, where my ancestors resided in Dubuque, was a tight-knit community. They were part of the group of residents referred to as the Northenders, since they were on the north side of Dubuque at the time. In census reports for this time, it is interesting to note that on that street were people not just from Germany at large but from the same area within Germany—Jugesheim, Hesse-Darmsdt. I am reminded of a quote by Bess Streeter Aldrich: "There is something satisfying and stabilizing in childhood to be surrounded by many relatives whose roots lie deep in a single community."[29]

German influence on American life included traits and activities like loving nature and enjoying comfortable picnics and Sunday strolls. These German immigrants were known for their consumption of beer, wine, or schnapps at family gatherings that included dancing, singing, and public feasting. The local taverns were the center for social meetings in the German community. I remember hearing that at one time Dubuque had the distinction of boasting the highest per capita consumption of alcohol anywhere in the world.

The Weitz Tavern on 22nd Street would have added complicity to that consumption. "It was once said that Dubuque either had a bar or a church on every corner."[30] That is obviously an exaggeration, but the city did have many of each. Sadly, still today Dubuque has one of the highest rates of alcohol abuse in the country.[31]

Alois Otto Weitz, The Weitz Tavern at 201 E. 22nd St., in the late 1930s.

I wasn't personally familiar with the Weitz Tavern, as it had gone out of business several years before I was born. My father didn't talk about growing up next door to the bar, at least not to me, though I have no doubt he did his share of helping with the business. Possibly he didn't talk about it due to his personal struggles as an alcoholic. My grandfather, Alois Otto, died at the age of 60, when my father was twenty-four years old. Four years later my grandmother died by suicide, having drunk what they thought was Lysol and thrown herself down the basement stairs. My father was still living at home at the time and was the one who found her; she then died in the arms of my Uncle John. The family had their share of hardship. A year later Dad married and began his own family.

Returning to the contributions Germans made to American life, there were others. The first kindergartens in the United States were established by Germans. Adding gymnasiums and physical education to schools was also an idea they brought. "They also introduced popular foods such as hotdogs, hamburgers, pretzels, strudel, sauerkraut and lager beer"[32] and were influential in a variety of fields. They carried the tradition of the printing industry to America, and "the first Bible in America was published in German by Christopher Saur, a German printer in Philadelphia in 1743."[33]

Johannes Guttenberg invented movable type in 1440,[34] and, as printing had originated in Germany, it is reasonable to assume that it would have been a popular trade both in Germany and among German immigrants to the USA. Dubuque had three German newspapers by 1856. Germans were also influential in introducing to their new homeland traditions like the Christmas tree and Santa Claus.

Even with all that was positive from the German culture, difficult times came during which anti-German sentiment would grow. I have always thought it a good thing that my ancestors were able to leave Germany before chaotic times arose there. 1917 and the war with Germany proved to be a setback for the German Americans, and circumstances changed for them in many ways.

There was discrimination, and German language newspapers were either closed or run out of business. Names of streets, towns, and foods were changed. At some point the street name Couler was changed to Central, and Sanford (the street the Weitz tavern was on) was changed to 22nd Street. German books were banned, and the teaching of German as a language was discontinued.

The anti-German attitude did ease in that many who went to fight against Germany were German American. "On May 14th, 1919, veterans of the Iowa 168th Infantry of the Rainbow Division returned home from France. Sixty-seven Dubuquers died, about half [of whom] were German Americans."[35]

WWII began twenty years later, and anti-German feelings redeveloped. The Nazi party came to power in 1933 and caused Germans and other Europeans to flee. The backlash in America wasn't as intense this time, however, and "the loyalty of German Americans was not questioned as virulently."[36] Due to war and the fact that many of German descent helped the United States in those struggles, they were assimilated into this country.

Not all people of German descent in America were supportive of America during this time, however. A Dubuquer by the name of Frederick Wilhelm Kaltenbach sympathized with the Germans. Born in Dubuque on March 29, 1895, Kaltenbach became a teacher at Senior High School in the late thirties. I learned of Kaltenbach from the book *The Old Lady in Dubuque* by Albert Kwasky. This book was written in response to an editor for the magazine *The New Yorker* by the name of Harold Ross. Ross made a claim that the magazine was not intended for "the old lady in Dubuque." In other words, it targeted a more "sophisticated" readership.[37]

I acquired a signed copy of this book, in which Kwasky sets out to identify just who the editor may have been referring to. One of the chapters is a recounting of Kwasky's own contact with Kaltenbach at the local YMCA. At this time the YMCA provided young men an opportunity to play chess while they waited for their hair to dry after showering and before going out into the cold. Kwasky and Kaltenbach played a couple of games, with the first ending in a draw and Kwasky winning the second; this outcome angered Kaltenbach, as he was the teacher and Kwasky a young student. It goes without saying that, had Kaltenbach won, Kwasky probably wouldn't have written about it.

Kaltenbach not only sympathized with Nazi Germany but promoted the ideology among his students, who were led like "a troop of super-charged Boy Scouts."[38] Kwasky describes going into Kaltenbach's school room, where on the walls was "an oversized road map of Germany; an American flag was up as a decoy, for underneath was a studio portrait of Adolf Hitler, brush mustache and all; and a painting scene of the Rhineland and German castles."[39]

I now wonder what my dad and his siblings thought about Kaltenbach, since they attended Senior High School at this time. An aside about my Uncle John: in 2002 he was inducted into his High School Sports Hall of Fame. The Dubuque Senior High School Sports Hall of Fame was created under the direction of my cousin Dick Weitz, who was an assistant principal and activity director from 1988 through 1996. John was inducted for his play during the 1937–38 football season and was coached by Wilbur Dalzell, who had earlier coached the very first recipient of the Heisman Trophy, Jay Berwanger. The trophy has an image of Berwanger running with the ball (the Heisman pose).

Dalzell himself held the distinction of being the first prep coach named to the Coaches' Hall of Fame in three sports— football, wrestling, and track. He had also coached a distant relative of mine, Fred Gloden, who went on to play in the NFL for the Philadelphia Eagles.[40] Gloden was instrumental in promoting the idea of putting in substitutions during a football game, a welcome idea when a lot of the good players played both offense and defense.[41] Like many other players during this time (such as the famous football player Nile Kinnick), their careers were interrupted by WWII.[42]

To return to the discussion about Kaltenbach, I realized that there would have been some overlap in my father's and uncles' years at Dubuque Senior, and I doubt he had influence over my uncles. Kaltenbach led a group called the Militant Order of Spartan Knights, whose members participated in "rock climbing, hiking, wrestling, boxing, weightlifting, swimming, cave exploring, and marksmanship."[43]

Kaltenbach was questioned about this group because it seemed pro-Nazi, and he even had the boys wearing brown shirts. At a meeting to discuss his activities with the boys, he made anti-American comments that so enraged those in attendance that Kaltenbach got punched in the mouth, and others jumped on him. He was dismissed from his position on May 13, 1935. After having been fired he left for Germany, and while there he began short-wave radio broadcasts that were considered to be propaganda.

He married Dorothea Peters, one of Hermann Goring's aviation editors, and that gave him access to high level Nazi leaders. He was indicted along with seven other Americans for treason on July 26,1943. Although the US tried to find him, he was arrested by Russian combat troops in Berlin on June 14, 1945, and is said to have died of "natural causes" in October 1945 somewhere in the Soviet zone.[44]

Returning to the idea of the assimilation and contributions of German Americans during times of war, the participation of some of my relatives went back as far as the Civil War:

- Great Uncle John J. Weitz at age 19 enlisted on August 16, 1862. He served until 1864 and was transferred to the Invalid Corps on February 29, 1864.
- Uncle Richard Weitz served in the US Navy as a chief petty officer during WWII and in the Korean and Vietnam wars. His enlistment date was March 14, 1943, and he was discharged on April 28, 1966.
- Uncle John Weitz served as a sergeant in the US Air Force during WWII from 1941–45.
- Uncle Ralph Weitz served as a master sergeant in the US Navy during WWII from 1942–45.
- Brother Tom Weitz was an army specialist while seeing active duty as an airborne ranger, as well as a staff sergeant with the National Guard, 2nd BN/75th INF Ranger, from October 1978–October 1981.
- Brother Paul Weitz served in the US Army and the National Guard Army from September 1983–September 1986 and in the reserves from 1986–97. Serving as a medic during active duty and later as an electrical technician, he was honorably discharged as an E6 staff sergeant.

- Nephew Trent Moore, a West Point graduate who finished 16th in his class, served as a captain in the US Army during the Kosovo and Iraq wars from 2000–2005.
- Leonard Peter Weitz, a cousin to my father, served during WWII. Leonard entered the service on May 20,1942, and departed from the US on December 24, 1943.

Leonard was a private first class as part of the 339th Infantry 85th Division of the Army. During the Italian Campaign, in an effort to push north to reach Rome, there were four main engagements, each of which was led by various Allied forces. The fourth engagement lasted from May 11–18 and was the one that brought success in taking the hill. Leonard was killed in action on May 13,1944, at the age of twenty-seven at the Battle of Monte Cassino. Lieutenant General Mark Clark was moved to write, "The battle for Cassino was the most grueling, the most harrowing, and in one respect the most tragic, of any phase of the war in Italy."

Allied forces had 105,000 casualties, and the Germans suffered 80,000 casualties.[45] There is a monument at Sicily-Rome at the American cemetery and a memorial where these veterans are interred. Leonard Peter Weitz's family received his Purple Heart Medal. (This medal, the oldest US military honor, was first called the Badge of Military Merit and was originally conferred by Washington in 1782. It is now awarded to anyone wounded or killed in any action against an enemy of the United States.)[46]

At the Veterans Memorial Park in Dubuque there is a paver with the above names listed, not including Leonard's. My brothers are also not listed, as they didn't see wartime service.

Italian Campaign, WWII Troops of the US Army's 85th Division (the division Leonard was a part of) marching through Port Maggiore as they occupy the city of Rome, June 5, 1944. US Signal Corps/National Archives, Washington, DC. The Purple Heart Medal photo is from the recipient, Rick Peters.

The Purple Heart in the picture above is not the one Leonard's family received but the one given to my brother-in-law, Rick Peters. Here is his story, as he tells it:

From an early age, all I wanted to do was be a Marine, so, when I graduated from high school in 1966 I talked my mom into signing my application. You had to be 18 to enlist, without needing a parent's signature, and I was 17 at the time. Being from west of the Mississippi, Marine boot camp is located in San Diego CA, so, I spent my 18th birthday in the receiving barracks. I was assigned to Platoon 3332, this was a platoon which contained all regular enlisted recruits. Our senior drill instructor was Staff Sargent Brennen. We also had two other drill Instructors.

Bootcamp was tough, lots of both physical and mental degrees of treatment, but, when you consider what was going on in the world, ie., Vietnam, it made sense to be as strict in our training as they could be. I loved it. In Marine Corps boot camp, platoons competed against each other for an award called "Honor Platoon" and is awarded to the platoon that excels in each phase of training. This includes, military history, physical activity, drill formation, swimming, inspection, rifle range, both rifle and pistol, hand to hand combat, jungle training, map and survival training, and amphibious landings. Well, being all regular Marines and knowing that we were going to be our senior drill instructor's last platoon, as he was going to be re-assigned, we, all together, worked our butts off and at graduation, we were awarded as an "Honor Platoon." It was a really big deal.

All of us came out of Boot camp as E-0 privates. After graduation, we received our orders as to where we would be sent. Most all of us were sent to Camp Pendleton, CA for further training, including an advanced combat program. I said most of us, but it depended on your MOS. This is your designated specialty in the Marine Corps. All infantry is 0311, basic rifleman. This was fine with me, I knew what I wanted and where I was going—Vietnam. I became Private First Class or E-1 at Camp Pendleton. In early March, 1967, my group left for California en route to Okinawa, Japan. There we were split up and sent to whichever outfit in Vietnam needed additional manpower. After we were assigned our unit we were flown to Da Nang, South Vietnam. From there I went by convoy to Chu Lai, South of Da Nang.

I was assigned to "Suicide Charlie" 1st Battalion 7th Marines, 1st Marine Division. As a "Newbie" in country, I had various duties. I carried a radio for a while, served as a rifleman for a while, went into a few tunnels, and just served my unit as needed. Our outfit spent most of the time out, away from base camp, and because of this we took several casualties. Combat activity was pretty high.

On the 8th of May, I was assigned to walking point for a recon patrol. It was around 1300 hrs. When we entered a small village, a check was made in each hut and, without finding any issues, we moved on. Ahead was a small cornfield, which was inside a horseshoe ravine. As I came out of the field and moved down into the ravine, my view was at level with the opposite side. As I started up and out, I was knocked down. I knew I had been hit,

I looked at my left arm and all I saw was blood, and my stomach was also bloody. The medic was on me very quickly and pulled me back into the ravine. I honestly thought I was going to die. All I could hear was gunshots and the medic yelling that he needed some help. I was moved back into the village and they worked to stabilize my wounds. As my squad members came back into the village, they kept telling me "we got them."

After initially treating me, I was transported to a MASH hospital. I was operated on and treated in the ward. I do remember laying on a hospital bed and looking at the person lying next to me—he only had one foot! I felt a little better then. I spent a couple days there, then moved to a naval hospital in Japan. I was moved to a MAC flight and sent to Scott Air Force Base in Illinois. I spent a short time there, then flew to Chicago and was sent to Great Lakes Naval Hospital. This was where I received my next rank increase to E-3 lance corporal. I had three more surgeries there and was moved to casual company. In January 1968 I was placed on the temporary disability list and given orders to report to the VA hospital in Iowa City, where I had two more surgeries. I finally was listed as an outpatient and just reported back as needed, but was still officially in the Marine Corps.

During the rest of 1968 I would go from the VA in Iowa City to Great Lakes and the VA in Des Moines. Each location would evaluate my injury and progress of recovery. The final outcome came on April 1st, 1970. I was awarded a medical retirement from the Marine Corps. What I had wanted—a career in the Marines—

came to a halt, from active duty anyway. And now you know the rest of the story."[47]

When I asked Rick to share and told him about my idea of including his story in this book, his response was that he would be honored. He also expressed that the process would bring back for him some painful memories but that he had been lucky to survive when others didn't. I assured him that the honor was mine and that we all need to hear about experiences like this, to be reminded of the sacrifices made. That is why communities set up memorials, and it is why we commemorate Veterans Day.

I remember when plans were being made for the Veterans Memorial Park and how excited my father was over its conception and completion. He let us all know about it. The plaza was established in 2009, and my sister was able to take him to its opening on Veterans Day, November 11, 2009. He passed away November 19, only eight days later.

The idea of the memorial was exciting to dad. He had never served in the military (he participated in ROTC as a cadet at Loras Academy), although I think he wanted to. He was appreciative of the sacrifices of others to secure and maintain our freedoms. Dad cared deeply about the political and moral issues we as Americans face. He could talk to anyone—he never met a stranger—and set a good example of a strong work ethic, as it was rare for him to miss work for sickness or for any other reason.

A term often used of a devout Catholic is "staunch," and that epitomized him. He never missed mass, though I remember one time while on vacation that he couldn't find a Catholic church, forcing us to attend a Protestant service. During Lent he would attend mass daily. Dad liked to sing and had done so in a church choir since he was eighteen years old, for a total of sixty-seven years.

I remember how he sought to teach us not to use profanity or take the Lord's name in vain. We were even scolded for using words like *gosh, gees, darn,* or *dang.* Those substitute swear words are known as minced oaths. His scolding didn't keep him from using the actual cuss words in his times of anger, however. Nothing screams hypocrisy more than someone saying, "Do what I say, not what I do"—which was a phrase he used. Overall, he meant well and did what he thought best for his family. Dad had his struggles with alcohol, and I remember crying myself to sleep after seeing him come home drunk one night. A stroke and a heart attack ultimately caused him to stop drinking.

Dad hanging out at one of the local establishments. Family album. Date unknown.

My father often wrote letters to the editor of the Dubuque paper, the *Telegraph Herald.* Most often he wrote on the subject of being pro-life, but also he wrote about anti-communism. Through several months of 1990 (I suppose because my mother was deceased) he seemed to write more frequently. He would bestow a monthly award on an individual or individuals—a "Golden Gaffe" award for something said or done that was embarrassing or a blunder. My, how busy he would have been in granting those awards with today's political figures!

In one letter to the editor, in response to comments Vice President Quayle had made about the absence of a father in the home, he wrote, "A most important lesson to be taught in strengthened homes is that individuals should come to believe as heretofore that the most prized civil possessions are encased in the Bill of Rights, the first 10 amendments to the Constitution. Everybody knows these include their right to freedom of assembly, freedom of the press and speech, and to bear arms, to name a few."[48] He went on, "The most important life threatened is not our way of life but life of the pre-born child. The abortion issue is not 'when does life begin?' Children now know life begins at conception. It has no place in the thinking of a pretentious political official, political activist, and guest editorialist."[49]

Dad wasn't alone in his strong pro-life position in our home. My mother also stood strong against abortion as a charter member and volunteer at Birthright, Inc. Birthright is an organization that offers an alternative to abortion. When my mother was on call, she would answer questions and provide love and support. I recall overhearing conversations she had with people that were technically confidential, but I could always tell from her side what the dialogue was about. Birthright sought to provide whatever was needed by way of testing and housing, as well as to deal with maternity issues and supply baby items.

Birthright began in Toronto, Ontario, Canada, in 1968. Keep in mind that this was before *Roe v. Wade* became law in the US and before the services of crisis pregnancy centers became an option.

My mom's work with Birthright was on a volunteer basis. Mom was always there for us. She was a kind, giving, patient person. Mom went to school for nursing, but she waited until the youngest of us kids was a junior in high school before she went back to work, despite having health needs of her own. Nursing served her and us well as she never panicked when we had our share of accidents and injuries.

It was in 1973 that *Roe v. Wade* was decided, along with Doe v. Bolton, opening the door for abortion on demand. I was in elementary school at the time, but I remember watching some of the proceedings with my parents and discussing the issue. My parents made it clear to me that life begins at conception. I would have loved to hear their thoughts when, on June 24, 2022, *Roe v. Wade* was overruled.

The Dobbs ruling stated that "the Constitution does not confer a right to abortion: Roe and Casey are overruled: and the authority to regulate abortion is returned to the people and their elected representatives."[50] It is interesting to note that even someone who supported women's right to choose was critical of the Roe decision—that being Supreme Court Justice Ruth Bader Ginsberg, who died in 2020. She believed that Roe focused on a right to privacy and not on women's rights.[51]

The reaction to Roe being overturned was varied. Some thought it meant the end of abortion in this country, and some states had trigger-bans in place, laws that would automatically take effect if Roe no longer applied. Without getting into specifics of where specific states landed, or the fact that at times resolutions will be placed on state ballots, it is important to see that the Dobbs decision would mean that babies would potentially be saved.

I realize that this is a heavy and emotional issue—please don't let that deter you from reading further. So much more could be said, and this issue is vital to where we are as a nation. I view the position my parents took on abortion as an example of the influence parents can have in helping to shape our views. But our lives are shaped by more than just these instilled values—there is also the aspect of where we grow up. As noted, for me that was Dubuque.

CHAPTER 4

DUBUQUE

recognize that venturing into some detail of my growing up in Dubuque and young adulthood is a bit of a detour from the main thrust of this book and the consideration of the pursuit of US citizenship. I share it because it brings me joy, and hopefully resonates with you. Knowing that our lives are tied to being an American citizen based on birthright is a cherished reality that is made possible by those who came before us. Similar stories could be told by successive generations of naturalized citizens from communities all over the country. That said, here are some memories of my childhood and early adulthood:

Where to start in telling you about my hometown? I think I will begin by telling you how, at a young age, I learned to spell the city name. I didn't learn it from my parents or siblings but from a commercial for Dubuque Meat. No, not the one with the dancing hams (Google it). Rather, it was the commercial that preceded that one. "D-U-B-U-Q-U-E spells Dubuque, the meat for your family. Look for the bright red fleur-de-lis, the symbol of flavor and quality." If you know it, you are now singing it. If only I had learned to put other facts I needed to learn to music in the same way, maybe I could have been a better student.

The city of Dubuque was given the name from one of the first white men to settle in the area, Julien Dubuque, in 1785. Julien was a Canadian born French fur trader who was granted rights to mine lead by the Meskwaki (sometimes spelled Mesquakie) Native Americans. It is believed that he took as a wife an Indian (Native American) woman by the name of Potosa.

"Dubuque built two furnaces to refine lead ore; one furnace was near Eagle Point Park, and the other at the mouth of Catfish Creek."[52] He gave the settlement the name "Mines of Spain." Mining became the means of prosperity for the city from 1833 to 1857 (1855 being the year my great-great-grandfather came to Dubuque).

Julien had died on "March 24th 1810, and was buried and honored in an elaborate ceremony by his Indian friends."[53] His grave is marked by a monument built in 1897 on a bluff overlooking the Mississippi River and Catfish Creek in the Mines of Spain Recreation Area. It is a bluff thought by some to be "the most picturesque spot on the Mississippi River."[54] With the draw of mining the lead deposits, as well as of the Mississippi River, immigrants began to arrive in the area.

The US government opened the land for settlement on June 1, 1833. The city of Dubuque was chartered in 1837, becoming Iowa's oldest city. Dubuque is located on the eastern side of Iowa, alongside what is said to be one of the finest rivers in the world. The "Mighty Mississippi" is a principal waterway that divides all, or parts, of thirty-one states in the heartland of the nation. Its name is from what the Chippewa called *mici zipi*, or "large river." Standing on the bank of the river in Dubuque and looking across the river, with your right eye you can see across to Illinois, and with your left eye you are looking at Wisconsin.

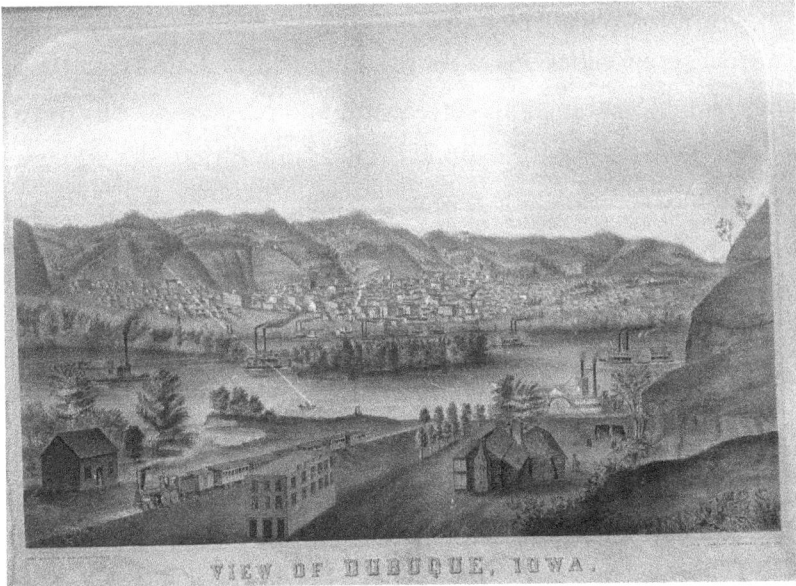

View of Dubuque lithograph on paper 1856 by Lucinda Farnham. Hanging at the Center for Dubuque History at Loras College.

The area is marked by hills and high bluffs. The city of Dubuque is now a destination for tourism. The city today has draws that were not always there: the major river front improvements didn't happen until after I had left Dubuque. The 1980s were a bit rough, but community leaders came together from private and public sectors to bring about change. The area by the river is now known as the "Port of Dubuque, in which there is a river walk, river museum and aquarium, Grand Harbor Resort and Star Brewery."[55] Prior to development and revitalization the area was an underutilized, industrial brownfield property. The city slogan is "Masterpiece on the Mississippi."[56]

The city has other features that are of interest. The list includes the Fourth Street Elevator, the Shot Tower, art museums, architectural districts, parks, and hiking and bike trails. It also boasts a nice downtown area. Sitting in what is appropriately called "Town Clock Plaza" is the town clock. I always thought the clock looked incomplete—as if it had been sawed off—or, as Albert Kwasky put it, "chopped down and sitting like a gnome plumb in the center atop a water fountain."[57]

The Town Clock Plaza was not the original location for the clock, which was initially placed atop the John Bell and Company building in November 1864, having been purchased in July of 1864 for $304.00. "The clock was said to keep the most accurate time of any clock in the United States."[58] The reason for its relocation was that it tumbled down in 1872.

A couple of issues led to its crash to the street. First was the excavation for a new building being constructed next door. As its foundation was being placed, workers noticed cracks appearing in the walls of the town clock building. They shouted a warning and took cover. The second reason was that the Bell building was not strong enough for the clock's 3,400-pound weight. It was an awful calamity, and two women and a child died as the building and clock collapsed. The time was 5:16 p.m. Saturday, May 25, 1872. The city decided to replace the clock, which began operating again in 1873. In 1971 the city decided to relocate the clock to its current location.

The Town Clock is precisely the spot at which my Aunt Margaret Winders passed away on May 19, 1985. Margaret loved to square dance—not only for herself but to bring joy to others. It was during a Dubuquefest, while on the Town Clock stage, after she had just finished a dance with Rose's Ramblers that she collapsed. Previous comments made by her included, "Well, you know, I'd be happy to die dancing for others," and "I love the Rose's Ramblers; they are my family. I hope I can die with them around me." Margaret was a childless widow, so it was nice for her to have people in her life she thought of as family. She was granted that desire May 19 at 4:30 p.m. on the Town Clock stage. Forgive the pun—her time had come.

Dubuque Town Clock. Picture taken by the author. September 2024.

As stated, the improvements happened after I moved from Dubuque. After high school I went to college at the University of Northern Iowa. For several years I missed family and Dubuque, especially in the fall. It was the changing of the leaves and the fall foliage I missed. The fall changes bring out the yellow of the sugar maples, cottonwood, hackberry, elm, basswood, and walnut trees, as well as red and orange from the Virginia Creeper and the sumac. The vibrant colors are beautiful against the backdrop of the limestone bluffs.

If you are from Dubuque, you referred to it as Dubuqeland, and you are a Dubuquer. That doesn't work for all hometowns. Now, I offer a glimpse of what growing up was like for me, I grew up in a large family, as already mentioned. I wasn't very good at making friends at a young age because, with brothers, I already had someone to play with. As I got older it became easier, once I overcame the initial difficulty, to make friends because many other families also had a lot of children. What it took was a brother telling me to "Go get your own friends" when I wanted to hang with him and his friends. Some of those friends from school and the neighborhood were the Vises, the Schwartzes, and the McDonells, to name a few. The rest know who they are. I would guess that, for many, this mention will trigger forgotten memories.

Nostalgic reminiscences are usually fun for everyone. I won't share a lot of detail here; my varied recollections are like rapid-fire vignettes. Some of these "memories" are the result of asking family members, "What was your favorite thing about growing up in Dubuque?" Also note that I don't use any particular order, though much of the material falls into seasonal categories.

Spring/summer: We were "free range kids" who ran loose as hoodlums in the neighborhood. There was no such thing as "helicopter parenting." Parents were in charge, and you were told when to be home, and that was it. We had freedom to ride our bicycles pretty much wherever we wanted, which was not always easy on Dubuque hills. Activities included lots of swimming at the City Municipal Pool, DQ stops on the way home, swimming in the Mississippi, fishing, Cub Scouts/Boy Scouts, a week at

Dubuque YMCA camp, hiking, hunting rabbits and squirrels in the woods and at the cemetery, canoeing, camping, drive-in theaters, and family vacations—for a stretch of years visiting relatives in Minnesota; either we would go there or they would come to Dubuque.

That family had nine children as well, so our gatherings made for a full house and fun times: making skateboards using old roller skates, building go-carts, shooting BB guns, BB gun fights in the cemetery (with winter coats on so it wouldn't hurt), placing pennies on the railroad tracks to smash them, water skiing, picnics (Eagle Point Park), assembling model rockets from a kit (painted and launched with an igniter), model cars, making forts by digging a huge hole and covering it with branches, treehouses, city parks, baseball, playgrounds (Burden Park), playing box hockey, delivering newspapers, mowing lawns, checking out books from the book mobile, holidays like the Fourth of July (when if you thought of it first you got to be the one to go out the bedroom window out onto the roof of the porch and hang the flag).

There was also the year (1978) when Sylvester Stallone came to town for the filming of the movie *F.I.S.T.* I got to shake his hand as he worked his way down the street. It was a big deal because it was in 1976 that the movie *Rocky* was released, and I remember doing workouts to the theme music from the movie. In 1976, as it was the nation's bicentennial year, the city sponsored the painting of fire hydrants in patriotic themes. We painted the one across the street from our home.

I also don't want to forget about a particular smell of summer—that being the mayfly swarms (or, as we called them, fish flies) that flocked to the lights of lamp posts and store signs.

They live for only twenty-four hours, and their dead bodies, which gathered in piles, smell like dead fish. I've read that there are swarms so large that they can be seen on radar.

My brother Tom, who has spent a good share of time on the river canoeing, kayaking, and dragon boat racing (Google it), tells of a time when he was on the river at night. They needed to have a light, but the light attracted the mayflies. There were so many that if they opened their mouths they would have flown in. They ended up with a pile of mayflies in the boat. I guess they are part of the food chain, as the emerging larvae and adult mayflies are food for crappie, perch, bass, and trout. They say that smells can trigger memories better than anything else, but that smell is one I can do without.

In summary, of these two seasons with all we had to do, it is hard to imagine that we at times claimed boredom, ended up rough housing, and had Mom threaten to send us to Boys Town. (If you're not familiar with Boys Town, it began in 1917 as a way to help homeless boys in Omaha, Nebraska. It was started by Father Edward Joseph Flanagan. The organization now has several locations across the country helping troubled youth, both boys and girls, and families).[59]

Fall/winter: Football in the clearing between the Mt. Calvary and Linwood cemeteries. Games in the neighborhood—like chase, which was a form of hide and seek fanning out across several neighborhood blocks; raking leaves and then gathering as many as you could, including from other yards to make a huge pile to jump in; Halloween—your costume being one of those plastic sweaty masks, or you dressed as a bum; basketball (renting the gym at Mt. St. Francis); raiding the apple orchard and grapes at Mt. St. Francis (sometimes we asked permission); throwing tomatoes or snowballs at vehicles from the vantage point of a bluff because you felt you always had an escape if the victims were to pursue; roller rink; go-cart track, sledding/tubing; or ice skating at Comiskey Park.

(Comiskey was originally called Olinger Park and was purchased by the city in 1928. It was a professional baseball park named after Charles Albert Comiskey, who played for the Dubuque Rabbits. Comiskey was a successful player, manager, and owner of the Chicago White Sox.)[60] There were also birthdays celebrated, but the celebration usually wasn't elaborate due to six of the nine of us having been born in September (cold winters must have brought my parents together, or maybe it was the holidays . . .).

Did I mention that each of us kids was born/brought into the world by a stork? It is true—Dr. Robert D. Storck, MD, lived up to his name since he spent a good part of his career delivering babies. Dr. Storck lived to the age of ninety-four and died in 2013. My family didn't have birthday celebrations, but my parents made up for it at Christmas. Christmas revolved around the tradition of having the tree and presents show up for the first time on Christmas morning so that we could all wake up to the splendor. That was made possible because the older kids stayed up to help set it all up.

A couple of other shenanigans, not necessarily revolving around fall and winter, come to mind. One involved going to the attic, getting one of Mom's old purses, and tying fishing line to the handle. We would throw it to the middle of the street and, when someone stopped to pick it up, reel it in—unseen because we hid behind the wall of the porch. Another antic entailed a group of us walking down the street at dusk; when a car approached we would divide ourselves onto opposite sides of the street and go through motions making it appear as if we had a rope between us. Our goal was to stop the traffic so we could laugh at the duped drivers.

Silly, innocent fun. I am sure there were many other puerile tricks and activities my siblings could add to this list. I remember hearing about kids lighting a bag of poop on fire at an unliked neighbor's front door in the hope that they would step out to stomp on it and get their shoes—or, better yet, their bare feet—full of poop. I only heard about that one and didn't participate.

There were plenty of other antics in my formative years that were not classified as innocent fun. I went through a stretch of years during which the friends I chose were negative influences. We all thought it was cool to smoke, and there were times when the smell from that activity was evident on me, but I lied and said it was my friends, not me, who had been smoking.

Exposure to pornography at an early age was another corrupting influence for me and some friends. Along those lines, there was abuse in our home that fed sensual desires. This contributed to my brothers and me thinking of the opposite sex as objects of our desires—which dominated much of my thinking. No wonder school and homework were never a priority. I was always one to get only average grades in school.

When my high school years rolled around, the one and only sport in which I was determined to participate was wrestling. I was mediocre at that as well. I thought that if I did all right my senior year, I would use that to help me decide where to go to college and give wrestling a try at that level.

Wrestling is popular in the state of Iowa. For several years, starting at an early age, I followed the University of Iowa wrestling program. Coach Dan Gable has always been a hero of mine. Naturally, I was excited when a nephew, Cliff Moore, competed and finished as a national champion for the University of Iowa in 2004. During my first year at the University of Northern Iowa I gave wrestling a try but ended up having problems that hindered me, like mononucleosis. Besides, I recognized that I wasn't good enough for that level. I did win a couple of intramural championships, though.

I decided to focus more on academics but still was not a very good student. During those first years of college, I came in contact with a couple of people who affected my thinking. A Campus Crusade worker did a gospel presentation with me, but I made up my mind (at that time, at least) that I was fine with how I had been raised and defended Catholicism. Another individual was a guy who handed out anti-war and arms race pamphlets. I almost became a conscientious objector, or at least a pacifist. I had a talk with my dad, though, and he was able to help me realize that my going that direction was exactly what Communists and anti-Americans would have wanted. It ended up being good that I discontinued my involvement with this individual, as he ended up having legal problems over his protests on campus.

The 1981–82 college year was a time of major change in my life. For my sophomore year I decided I wanted to live with some friends off campus. At one point I came across a friend I had made from the dorms the year before. Mark had also been raised a Catholic but had recently become a Christian. Mark shared his newfound faith with me and invited me to meetings held by a group called Campus Bible Fellowship (CBF). I took him up on his invitation.

While at one of the meetings I heard a message on evangelism. I wrote down on the message handout that Christ had died for my sins, had been buried, and rose again (1 Corinthians 15:3–8).

The speaker, Hal Miller, also pointed out the difference between knowing facts about Jesus and believing in Him. He used the analogy of the way a person can know about a past President, let's say Abraham Lincoln. You can know that he lived and died, but you can't believe in someone who is dead. Given the resurrection of Christ, you can believe in Him, since He is alive.

For several nights after that I would pick up that paper, look at what I had written, and think, *If this is what I need to believe, then that is what I want.* After attending another meeting on campus, I was asked by a campus worker from the group if he could stop by my apartment and talk. I was willing. When a couple of guys from the staff of the CBF ministry, Tom and Hans, stopped by, they shared more Scripture with me. It was interesting that Hans had been a wrestler at UNI who'd had his career cut short due to injury.

Incidentally, this was the third time I'd had contact with believers who also had a connection to wrestling. One encounter had taken place the year prior, when CBF had an Olympic champion wrestler, Ben Peterson, as a speaker. It was at this meeting that, as a result of their contact with me, CBF leaders began to pray for me. It was a few years later that I came across a notebook that listed prayer requests with my name as one of the people being prayed for.

The second encounter occurred when I was introduced to a man named Butch while I was hanging out at a bar near campus. Ironically, Butch had also wrestled for UNI. He came back to our apartment and spent a couple of hours sharing his faith with us. Of course, the third time was with Hans. It is incredible to me to look back and be amazed that God used an interest in the sport of wrestling to draw me to Himself.

It was on a Thursday evening, April 1, 1982, when for the first time I recognized myself as a sinner in need of a Savior. I had done things in my life that I knew to have been wrong. There was the drinking, although that wasn't a huge problem for me, but also immorality, etc. I realized that there were aspects of my life that I couldn't change on my own. The truths shared with me that night began to make sense. I recall that Tom spoke of fulfilled prophesy regarding the birth of Christ, and I asked him a question: "What is going to happen between me and my dad if I become a Christian?" Tom, who was always wise, replied, "That is something that in time you will deal with. The question is, What are you going to place your faith in?"

Thus began a time of both change and challenges. I didn't make a break from Catholicism right away. During the spring and summer months, because of my need of a job, I was away from the influence of that group of Christians. What I did do was work through a Bible study via correspondence with Tom. I also began to read as much of the Bible as I could. It was during this time that I began to see contradictions between what the Bible says and what the Roman Catholic Church teaches. (A listing of how biblical Christianity differs from Catholic teaching is beyond the scope of this book.)

The college year to follow was one of involvement with CBF meetings; Bible studies; and attendance at a solid, Bible-believing church where I was baptized. I got to meet and date Crystal, who said Yes when I asked her to marry me. We had first gotten together on Valentine's Day in 1984, became engaged on the next Valentine's Day, and were married on August 17, 1985.

During our first year of marriage we made a move to Ankeny, Iowa, where I attended Bible college. I did that for one year and then began work in the area (Des Moines). Our lives have had various challenges. One of those struggles involved finding out about my infertility, the outcome for me being grief over the loss of a loved one I would never know. Yes, not the grief of losing a child, but a grief nevertheless. We had thought we would like to have up to four children. (We ended up taking the route of adoption and have been blessed with two great children. Some of that is a story for another time.) We also hit times of marital struggles, which by God's grace we made it through.

★ ★ ★

We have covered some about my ancestors, Dubuque life, and my own life. Now I would like to deal with the place at which I see us currently as a nation, followed by some thoughts on immigration and citizenship. Finally, I'll conclude with the biblical idea of citizenship.

CHAPTER 5

COMMUNISM

I have frequently wondered about communism taking a foothold in our country. I have asked myself, If there were to be a prevailing world political ideology in what Christians understand to be the "end times," would that prevailing ideology be communistic in nature? Meaning, would our nation no longer be a constitutional republic and fall under authoritative rule? America seems to be going in that direction no matter which political party is in power. Sadly, it is a direction that has veered us as a nation far from the principles and values of our founders. For the sake of citizenship there is a need to recognize that communist nations don't provide their people freedom, for which many have fought and died for.

Sometimes a good way to appreciate what you have is to contrast it with what others have. Many are becoming convinced that socialism and communism are a good thing, without taking an actual look at what they are really all about. Communism is ushered in by creating chaos and revolution, and then it promises a brighter future. Along the way there is propaganda and control. With state ownership and control, the average citizen has no individual rights; everything is for the sake of the collective. The communist system suppresses freedom. Freedom of speech, freedom of press, and freedom of assembly are nonexistent. The Chinese Communist Party (CCP) for decades pushed a one-child policy on their people. There is no private ownership of land, as it is all owned by the state, along with corporations. Even churches are state controlled as the system is atheist anyway. Finally, there now exists a means for keeping their citizens in check with a social credit system. This system collects data and rewards or punishes based on compliance with laws and other factors.

As we see the loss of freedoms and have a disregard for the Constitution and the Bill of Rights, would a form of communism take hold here? We see a disintegration of societal institutions and the things that build a strong nation. We have lost our way, and much of that has seemed intentional. Don't be mistaken, there is still a lot of good about the US and a lot to be thankful for. To cover all aspects of where we are headed and who is behind it would require another book. There are numerous books and resources available to gain knowledge about our country, and I lack the qualifications to be an authority; I view myself simply as a concerned citizen. As such, I see the need for our citizens to better understand our founding and the basis of what distinguishes us as a nation.

There is much debate and rewriting of history with regard to the influence Christianity had on the founding of this nation. While there is no such thing as a "Christian nation" in an earthly sense, we are a nation that was in its inception influenced by Judeo-Christian values. Despite a Supreme Court Decision in 1892, Church of the Holy Trinity v. United States, "this is a Christian nation."[61] Within this decision regarding the migration of foreigners coming into the US for religious work, examples of charters, constitutions, and declarations describing religious and Christian views were referenced.

In this regard, it was helpful for me to read the book *Did America Have a Christian Founding? Separating Modern Myth from Historical Truth* by David Hall. "When it comes to the Constitution," Hall writes, "It is necessary to consider the ideas that influenced the civic leaders who drafted and ratified the document. When one does so, it is clear that Christian commitments played an influential—even dominant role—in the drafting and ratification of the Constitution."[62]

One of those individuals was John Adams; Hall further quotes Adams as saying, "Referring specifically to the US Constitution he wrote in 1798 that 'our Constitution was made for a moral and religious people. It is wholly inadequate to the government of any other.'"[63] The ideas behind the Declaration of Independence and the Constitution included man being created in the image of God and our rights being derived from Him. Since those rights come from Him and are not granted by a human government, these early Fathers were led by that understanding to include provision for checks and balances in government because they understood the tendency of men to abuse power.

Hall states, "Like Lord Acton, they were convinced that 'power tends to corrupt, and absolute power corrupts absolutely.'"[64] The founders understood that adding checks and balances (the executive, legislative, and judicial branches of the American government) could help prevent tyranny.

The question we now need to ask is whether we are still functioning with the checks and balances in place, considering the size of our government, the state of its administration, and the use of executive orders. For a review of the administrative state, I found an article by Ron Pestritto to be helpful. In "The Birth of the Administrative State: Where It Came from and What It Means for Limited Government," Pestritto traces the beginning of the administrative state to Woodrow Wilson.

Wilson got this thinking from German authors of the Hegelian tradition.[65] Basically, it is the progressive notion that the Constitution is outdated and that it's better to have the "experts" of the administration set rules and regulations separately from politics, with the thought that this will improve efficiency. Bear in mind that these are unelected and unaccountable agencies. It may be that during Wilson's time one could trust the core to be patriotic, freedom-loving Americans, but it may be argued that that isn't the case anymore.

Keep in mind that our nation was established as a republic. Besides the three branches, we have what could almost be considered a fourth branch of government: that is, the individual and the people. Being a republic means that we have a representative form of government—which is not the same as a democracy, though our system of government is now constantly being referred to as such with statements like, "Such and such is a threat to our democracy." A democracy would simply be a nation that has elected officials and majority rule. If we agree that we are no longer a republic, we have to wonder what happened and when did that transition take place. Can and will we pivot back to being more of a republic?

I would venture to say that there are a variety of answers to those questions. Is the change due to an administrative state that has inflated the size of government? We have, as I have noted, an administrative state that develops and enforces rules and regulations by unaccountable, unelected officials. Or is it due to our having elected officials who are out for self-interest and the maintaining of power and not serving the interests of the people they represent? Or is this shift due to a lot of those elected officials being concerned with the interests of lobbyists such as pharmaceutical companies? Maybe it is due to the philosophy and ideas of some in government who no longer feel obliged to follow the Constitution, even though they took an oath to uphold it.

It is interesting to note in reading the Declaration of Independence how many of the matters over which the founders took issue with England and King George could also apply to modern America. The level of taxation is one example. Getting away from a just system of laws is another, with reference to our two-tiered justice system and to what some are now referring to as lawfare.

Allowing millions to cross the border illegally doesn't sound like the "promotion of the general welfare," being as this practice is unsustainable. Yes, I realize that those words appear in the Constitution and not in the Declaration of Independence, but both of these founding documents are being undermined.

Knowing what precisely our forefathers intended by their concern for the rights of the individual, the rule of law, and a representative government, I ask whether we are now living under a new form of tyranny? Are we losing the liberties they envisioned and fought for? While we consider the concept of functioning as a republic, as opposed to communism, or any other form of government, perhaps this is a good time for us not only to define that term but to consider other aspects that have, and will have, a determining influence on us as a nation and as individual citizens.

PART 2

PRESENT AND PROMISE

CHAPTER 6

COMING TO TERMS

" Coming to Terms"—this chapter title carries dual meaning. First, we need to understand the terms relevant to political systems, American and otherwise, that affect both would-be Americans and citizens of other nations. Second, if we have opinions that we may want to rethink, we will need to be honest and willing to adjust our thinking. It is possible to have genuine, fruitful discussion—and, yes—even arguments about these issues. Why and how did we ever come to the point that to differ means that one or the other or us has to be "unfriended" or "canceled" or even hated?

There are people—communists, for example—who do hate the freedoms and ideals that represent our nation. The communist doesn't just hate but is out to destroy. For a fuller understanding of this, I suggest Jesse Kelly's book *The Anti-Communist Manifesto*. He writes, "Whatever his vision for the future, he (the communist) believes America as constituted by the founders, stands in the way. At the center of all of it is an abiding hatred of his nation, her history, and the functions upon which she is built. That hatred unifies disparate groups that compose the modern communist movement."[66] Although this very brief statement does not in itself fully explain the whys and hows of the communists' thinking (reflecting only on the repercussions of applying their ideology), it does point to the importance of understanding a term. I would refer you to the definition of Communism later on in this chapter.

The decision to include the following information here, as opposed to in a "glossary of terms" in the back of the book, is to invite the reader to more seriously consider them. If this material seems to be cumbersome to read, at least review the list and consider what catches your eye. I took the time to explore and include this information due to its relevancy for citizenship in the United States, as well as in part to ensure that I, myself, would have a better idea of what a given term means, even if I do not fully comprehend it. Space isn't going to permit long or drawn out explanations; my intention in compiling the list was to consider terms and agencies that influence us as a nation and its citizens. The list is hardly intended to be exhaustive, and I invite you to conduct additional research on any of these terms as you deem beneficial.

1619 Project: understood by conservatives to be a journalistic rewriting of our history and an attack on the basis of America, its founding and growth. A new origin study published in 2021 claims that America's founding revolved around the beginnings of slavery—that our founding and the revolution were about protecting the institution of slavery. This theory was conceived by *New York Times* writers and developed by Nikole Hannah-Jones, who was originally from Waterloo, Iowa.[67] I see a need for balance in teaching, including the recognition of slavery as a factor in our founding, but that shouldn't lead to critical race theory—see the definition for CRT. Teaching that America is systemically racist and alleging that we are all either oppressors or victims inculcates a hatred for America.

Abortion: the termination of a pregnancy by removal or expulsion of a baby. Abortion is the termination of a pregnancy before the fetus can survive outside the uterus. It can occur spontaneously, known as a miscarriage, or be induced intentionally through medical or surgical procedures.[68]

Administrative state: the government structure that flows from executive branch administrative agencies believing that they are the experts, though they are made up of unelected, unaccountable bureaucrats who create, adjudicate, and impose rules and regulations (IRS, FDA, FBI, DOJ, etc).[69]

Agenda 2030: The United Nations has outlined 17 goals and objectives to end hunger, achieve gender equality, and combat climate change. This came about at their general assembly in 2005, and the aims are collectively referred to as Sustainable Development Goals. (This all sounds good, but in reality the United Nations wants control at the expense of our freedoms.[70]

Antisemitism: hostility toward, or discrimination against, Jews as a religious, ethnic, or racial group.[71]

Authoritarianism: blind submission to authority. The concentration of power in a leader or an elite not constitutionally responsible to the people. Similar to totalitarianism: centralized control by an autocratic authority; the political concept that the citizen should be totally subject to an absolute state authority.[72] In subjection there is no allowance for dialogue or debate. That is why censorship and propaganda are needed.

Autocracy: the authority or rule of an autocrat. Government in which one person possesses unlimited power.[73]

Border crisis (illegal immigration): a leading political issue with millions of illegal immigrants from a variety of countries coming across the US border. The problem taxes border control and the system. Human trafficking and fentanyl coming from China add to the problem.[74]

Capitalism: an economic and cultural system characterized by private or corporate ownership of capital goods by investments that are determined by private decision and by the prices, production, and distribution of goods that are determined mainly by competition in a free market.[75]

CBDC: Central Bank Digital Currency is a form of digital currency issued by a country's central bank.

Censorship: the institution, system, or practice of censoring. To censor is to examine in order to suppress or delete anything considered objectionable.[76]

CFR: Founded in 1921, the Council on Foreign Relations is an independent, nonpartisan think tank and publisher that promotes understanding of international relations and foreign policy.[77]

Christian Conservative: Such individuals, sometimes referred to as the religious right, are strongly in support of socially conservative and traditionalist policies (moral values, sanctity of life, and strong families and marriages). They have the desire to influence public policy with their understanding of Christianity.[78]

CRT—Critical Race Theory: considers racism to be systemic and alleges that there is unjust racism by white people, at the expense of people of color, increasing racial oppression. The theory divides people into victimizers and victims based exclusively on their race or ethnicity.[79]

Climate Change (Climate Crisis, Climate Alarmism, Global Warming): the idea that mankind is causing changes to the earth, beginning in the 1800s, due to fossil fuels that generate greenhouse gas that traps the sun's heat and raises the earth's temperature. In discussions on this subject, I like to point out that if everything scientists have told us about it were true, we wouldn't be here now. This also leads to the topic of geo-engineering, involving chem-trails that fill our skies in an effort to shield the earth from sunlight to keep temperatures low. What makes up the spray is not widely known, but based on studies of the soil it is aluminum, strontium, barium, and various concoctions of these. Most articles on the subject suggest that this is the result of a conspiracy theory. But what gives anyone the right to spray the skies? Why don't we have the right to know the truth about what is taking place? I would add here that we should care about the environment and be good stewards of our resources.

Communism: A totalitarian system of government by which there is a single authoritative party in control of the state-owned means of production. The system is said to be brought about by class struggle and conflict. Since that system precludes questions, there is no free speech. Historically, this system has been responsible for the deaths of millions.[80]

Conservatism: the principles and policies of a conservative party; a disposition to preserve what is established; a political philosophy that is based on tradition and social stability, stressing established institutions and preferring gradual development to abrupt change.[81]

Conspiracy theory: an explanation for a harmful or tragic event or situation that asserts the existence of a conspiracy by powerful and sinister groups, often political in motivation, when other explanations are more probable. Such explanations reject an accepted narrative. A convenient way to disregard something you don't want to believe is true. Conspiracy theory is different from a simple conspiracy, which is a covert plan involving two or more people.[82]

Constitutional republic: a nation in which, rather than directly governing, the people select some of their members to temporarily serve in political office as their representatives. Being constitutional means that both the citizen and their governing officials are bound to follow the Constitution. "A constitutional republic limits the power of the majority through a framework that promotes competent government and affords protections for fundamental rights".[83]

Deep State: a term that originated in Turkey in the 1990s when the military colluded with drug traffickers and hitmen to wage a war with Kurdish insurgents. It is a type of government made up of potentially secret and unauthorized networks of power, like active and retired members of the Justice Department together with other security agencies, operating independently of a state's political leadership in pursuit of their own agenda and goals.[84]

DEI—Diversity, Equity, and Inclusion: three closely linked ideas held by many corporations and organizations that are working to be supportive of different groups of individuals, including people of different races, ethnicities, religions, abilities, genders, and sexual orientations.[85] It results in filling quotas without consideration of merit and sometimes is a form of reverse discrimination.

Democracy: government by the people, especially rule of the majority.[86] Power is vested in the people and exercised by them and only reflected in a vote. The leaders and those they lead are not under a constitution and a set of rights such as the united States has.

Dictatorship: a form of government in which absolute power is concentrated in a dictator or a small clique.[87]

Election integrity: The right to vote in a secure, free, and fair election is a citizen's most basic civil right, the one on which many of the other rights of Americans depend. Simple solutions like photo identification and proof of US citizenship to prevent fraud are helpful.[88]

Electoral College: the group of presidential electors that is formed every four years for the sole purpose of voting for the President and Vice President of the United States. It is based on Article II of the US Constitution. The number of electors in each State is based on the number in that State's congressional delegation: one elector for each member in the House of Representatives and for each of the two Senators. The political left would like to change this system and rely strictly on a popular vote. The President needs a majority of 270 electoral votes to win an election.[89]

Elites: a small group of powerful people who hold a disproportionate amount of wealth, privilege, political power, or skill within a group.[90]

Environment, Social, and Governance (ESG): an index score[91] imposed by major corporations and businesses that benefits the so called "woke" (see definition further in this chapter) businesses and drives others out of business. It's a push toward sustainability that is similar to the Chinese style political system. The "Environmental" factor looks at a company's impact on the environment (climate change adherence), the "Social" evaluates a company's impact on society (DEI adherence), and "Governance" looks at a company's management and decision-making processes (managerial willingness to do all of the above).

Fake News: stories that are neither true nor real but that are often sensational in nature and created to be widely shared or distributed for the purpose of generating revenue or promoting or discrediting a public figure, political movement, company, etc.[92] Note that this is not the same as media bias, which is a slant given to a story or issue either toward the liberal or the conservative side.

Fascism: a political philosophy, movement, or regime that exalts nation, and often race, above the individual and stands for a centralized, autocratic government.[93]

Federal Reserve System: the central bank of the United States. Seeks to ensure financial stability; sets monetary policy; monitors financial system risks; promotes the safety and soundness of individual financial institutions; promotes a safe, efficient, and accessible system for US dollar transactions; and advances supervision, community reinvestment, and research to improve understanding of the impacts of financial services policies and practices on consumers and communities. Established by the

Federal Reserve Act signed by President Woodrow Wilson on December 23, 1913. Created in response to repeated financial panic.[94] It all sounds good and essential but, again, leads to greater regulation and control.

Free speech: included in the first amendment of the Bill of Rights as a fundamental right: "Congress shall make no law respecting an establishment of religion, or prohibiting the free exercise thereof; or abridging the freedom of speech, or of the press, or the right of the people peaceably to assemble, and to petition the Government for a redress of grievances."[95] There are exceptions to free speech—you can't incite imminent lawless action or use obscenity, defamation, or speech integral to criminal conduct, cannot promote child pornography or fraud or use speech presenting a grave and imminent threat. Along with this topic, consider the various forms of information. There is the simple presentation of facts. There is misinformation (something shared that is false and inaccurate), disinformation (created to manipulate and mislead a person), and mal-information (information spoken out of context to mislead, harm, or manipulate).[96]

Genocide: the deliberate and systematic destruction of a racial, political, or cultural group.[97]

Great Reset: set in motion by the World Economic Forum as a response to COVID-19 and climate change in 2020.[98] It is an agenda to change the world economically to a stakeholder rather than a shareholder economy and to create equality and sustainability and to "harness the innovations of the so called Fourth Industrial Revolution." The desire is to use modern technologies like AI, robotics, the internet of things, blockchain genetic engineering, and other technologies. Also involved is the switch to renewable energy like solar and wind to reduce carbon dioxide greenhouse effects.

Identity politics: political or social activity by or on behalf of a racial, ethnic, cultural, religious, gender, or other group, usually undertaken with the goal of rectifying injustices suffered by group members.[99] The usual outcome is strife and division.

Ideology: a systematic body of concepts, especially about human life and culture. The integrated assertions, theories, and aims that constitute a sociopolitical program.[100]

Indoctrination: instruction, especially in fundamentals or rudiments, teaching. To imbue with a usually partisan or sectarian opinion, point of view, or principle.[101]

Islam: the faith, doctrine, or cause of this religion. Islam is the religious faith of Muslims, as given in the Koran (Quran), including belief in Allah as the sole deity and Muhammad as his prophet.[102]

Left, the: the principles and views of the political left that can vary through time. The views that include economic, moral, social, historical, and environmental differences compared to the beliefs of the conservatives on the right. Synonyms include "left wing" and "liberalism," although these terms are not identical and can be differentiated.[103]

Liberalism: a political philosophy based on belief in progress, the essential goodness of the human race, and the autonomy of the individual, and standing for the protection of civil liberties.[104]

Libertarianism: advocating the doctrine of free will. Advocates uphold the principles of absolute and unrestricted liberty, especially of thought and action.[105] At first glance one could agree with some of the libertarian views since there is emphasis on individual rights, but there is a lack of acknowledgment of where those rights come from.

Liberty: the quality or state of being free, the power to do as one pleases, freedom from physical restraint, freedom from arbitrary or despotic control; and the positive enjoyment of various social and economic rights and privileges.[106]

Maoism: the theory and practice of Marxism-Leninism, developed in China chiefly by Mao Tse-tung.[107]

Marxism: the political, economic, and social principles and policies advocated by Karl Marx, especially a theory and practice of socialism, including the labor theory of value, dialectical materialism, the class struggle, and dictatorship of the proletariat until the establishment of a classless society.[108] I'll add that millions have been killed by its spread and that it is atheistic in worldview.

Media bias: occurs when journalists and news producers show bias (an inclination of temperament or outlook; prejudice) in how they report and cover news and issues. It takes various forms but is mostly seen in coverage bias and in false balance of coverage.[109]

Nazism: the body of political and economic doctrines held and put into effect by the National Socialist German Workers Party in the Third Reich; it espouses the totalitarian principle of government, state control of all industry, predominance of groups assumed to be racially superior, and supremacy of the Führer.[110]

New World Order: the idea that there are elites seeking to implement a totalitarian world government leading to one world leader with global control, including an across-the-world economic system.

Oligarchy: government by the few in which a small group exercises control, especially for corrupt and selfish purposes.[111]

Patriotism: love for or devotion to one's country.[112] Having a sense of patriotism is strongly tied to the way we view citizenship. Our conduct as a citizen can be represented in patriotic duty.

Progressivism: the principles and beliefs of progressives who believe in moderate political change and, especially, social improvement by government action; progress to move forward to develop a higher, better, more advanced stage.[113] This sounds like a good thing but implies more government control and regulation. In the US, it includes the idea that the Constitution is outdated.

Propaganda: the spreading of ideas, information, or rumors for the purpose of helping or injuring an institution, cause, or person. Ideas, facts, or allegations spread deliberately to further one's cause or damage an opposing cause.[114] Propaganda is also the promotion of a narrative, true or false, to help one's own cause. That is like rewriting the history of an event immediately after it happens. Over time propaganda can cause a conditioning effect on what a culture views as important.

Racism: the belief that race is the primary determinant of human traits and capacities and that racial differences produce the inherent superiority of a particular race; racial prejudice or discrimination.[115]

Revolution: a fundamental change in political organization, especially the overthrow or renunciation of one government ruler and the substitution of another by the governed.[116]

Right, the: people or groups that espouse conservative views, like limited government and lower debt. In contrast to the Left, who have liberal views and promote progressive reforms. There is a difference between the Right and the Radical Right that is extreme and ultraconservative and could endorse white supremacy and nationalistic views.

Secular humanism: the worldview that people through their own reason, logic, and determination can explain humankind's existence and future without theology and the supernatural. It is a philosophy rooted in pride and atheism, and it sees everything materialistically and as derived through evolutionary means.

Socialism: Any of the various economic and political theories advocating the collective of government ownership and administration of the means of production and distribution of goods. There is no private property under this theory, and the means of production are owned and controlled by the state.[117] Note that socialism is espoused in the claim that it will produce equality.

Technopolis: a society that is built on and has deified technology, seeks its authorization through technology, finds its satisfaction in technology, and takes its orders from technology (e.g., Amazon, Apple, Google, and Facebook).[118]

Transgenderism: an umbrella term for persons whose gender, identity, gender expression, or behavior does not conform to that typically associated with the sex to which they were born.[119]

Transhumanism: the position that human beings should be permitted to use technology to modify and enhance human cognition, bodily function, and brain-computer interface, thereby expanding abilities and capacities beyond current biological constraints.[120] Similar to AI in that, though there will be uses for good, there will be ethical questions as well. Ultimately, or course, there remains the reality of death regardless of the changes made.

Tribalism: a loyalty to or preference for one's own people. Cultural tribalism refers to the subdivision of society into groups that come together based on shared or specific types of thinking or behavior.[121]

Tyranny: oppressive power over the mind; oppressive power exerted by a government in which absolute power is vested in a single ruler.[122]

Woke: to have become aware of and actively attentive to societal facts and issues (especially issues of racial and social justice).[123] It is a liberal/progressive way to change society through ESG, CRT, climate alarmism, and gender ideology. The term goes back a long way to the early twentieth century and was originally used in the context of Black citizens in other countries. The term became a watchword for groups like Black Lives Matter following the killing of Michael Brown in Ferguson, Missouri, in 2014.

World Economic Forum: begun in 1971 with a history of collaboration of business, government, civil society, and stakeholders to bring about solutions to global issues. "It engages organizations and leaders through dialogue, debate and commitments for action in the service of building more future-ready, resilient, inclusive, and sustainable economies and societies."[124]

World Health Organization: Founded in 1948, WHO is a United Nations agency that connects nations, partners, and people to promote health, keep the world safe, and serve the vulnerable—so that everyone everywhere can attain the highest levels of health.[125]

CHAPTER 7

LIBERTY

The previous chapter lists and defines sixty-three terms and agencies and is included at least in part to assist individuals interested in pursuing the process of naturalization and attaining citizenship. You will notice that several of the definitions include notes or personal commentary. More could be added and more complete definitions and clarifications given. I experienced my own example of this when, after initially completing the list, I came across the word "dissident." A dissident is one who opposes the official policy of an established religious or political system, especially that of an authoritarian state.[126] That provides an example of how this list can change and grow.

The main idea of including this section is to enhance understanding and invite adjustments in our thinking if needed. Some of these terms have been the subject of whole books. I encourage additional research, debate, and intellectual honesty. We all need that because our thinking shouldn't be limited to whatever is reported or promoted in social media or on the nightly news. Similar to the transgender individual who decides at some point to de-transition, we may need to de-transition our minds. I am in no way making light of that process—this is just an analogy.

An example of someone who has changed her thinking is Tulsi Gabbard, author of *For Love of Country Leave the Democrat Party Behind*. Tulsi, a Democratic congresswomen from Hawaii, chronicles her switch after having served in the military, providing example after example of why she felt compelled to alter her allegiance. The Democratic party, she says, "is now under the complete control of an elitist cabal of warmongers fueled by cowardly wokeness who divide us by racializing every issue and stoke anti-white racism, actively work to undermine our God-given freedoms enshrined in our Constitution, are hostile to people of faith and spirituality, demonize the police and protect criminals at the expense of law-abiding Americans, allow our borders to remain open while claiming they are 'secure,' weaponize the national security state to go after political opponents, and, above all, drag us closer to nuclear war with each passing day."[127]

The issues Tulsi writes about are ones that should concern every American. The list in the previous chapter includes each of these, from abortion to the border crisis. Notice that no individuals are mentioned because the people currently involved will be subbed out. The people, plans, and programs will all change as time goes on.

I also believe that the direction we have taken to move away from being a Constitutional Republic isn't the doing of just one party. Neither party wants to take the path toward change that would regain loss of freedoms, provide us with a limited government, and return us to the rule of law. That is why what we have today in terms of political affiliation is often referred to as a uni-party.

With regard to loss of freedoms, we saw that happen in our response to the 9/11 attacks in 2001, when our government felt we needed to do something in response to the acts of terrorism committed. The Patriot Act was signed into law for the purpose of "intercepting and obstructing terrorism."[128] The act has, sadly, been used to target everyday, innocent citizens, resulting in privacy concerns and the abuse of civil liberties. I remember the discussions over loss of freedom versus safety during those days after 9/11. We did give up freedoms for safety—and we are reminded of this every time we go through airport security.

This reminds me that, at right around this same time I was reading the book *The Trumpet of the Swan* by E. B. White to my son. Toward the end of the book Louis the Swan gets an offer from the zookeeper to live out his days with all the benefits of staying in the zoo. Louis's response was, "Safety is all well and good, but I prefer freedom."[129]

You may protest, "That's the words of a swan in a fictional book." If so, then consider the words of Benjamin Franklin: "Those who would give up essential liberty to purchase a little temporary safety, deserve neither liberty or safety."[130] This quote from 1775 had to do with disagreements between the colonies and the crown, so not exactly the situation we face now. The point for us, though, is that any society that gives up freedoms for safety or security should know that this will lead to oppression and control over aspects of our lives.

There are also the words from a powerfully written book that contributed to this nation's Civil War. Harriet Beecher Stowe wrote *Uncle Tom's Cabin, or Life Among the Lowly*. Stowe began its writing in 1851 as a series of installments in an anti-slavery weekly publication, *The National Era*. The book was banned in many of the Southern states at the time for obvious reasons. *Uncle Tom's Cabin* gives the reader an idea of the terrible conditions of life for many of the slaves in the South, giving names and faces to the way some slaves were treated and abused as property of the owners.[131]

The book, though fictional, helped to galvanize the abolitionist movement. According to legend, Abraham Lincoln told her, "So you are the little woman who wrote the book that started this great war."[132] The book has been banned in modern times in some libraries and schools because of the use of the *N* word. That word was common at the time, used by slave owners and between slaves. It is today considered deeply offensive, however, and is often used to make Black people feel inferior and less than human.

It is possible that our culture frowns upon this book because of its emphasis on Christianity and maybe not so much because of the *N* word as because of the *L* word: *liberty*. Stowe beautifully writes about a slave family as they were making their way to freedom:

> Their night was far spent, and the morning star of liberty rose fair before them. Liberty; electric word! What is it? Is there anything more in it than a name—a rhetorical flourish? Why, men and women of America, does your heart blood thrill at that word, for which your Fathers bled, and your braver mothers were willing that their noblest and best should die?
>
> Is there anything in it glorious and dear for a nation, that it's not also glorious and dear for a man? What is freedom to a nation, but freedom to the individuals in it? . . . To your Fathers, freedom was the right of a nation to be a nation. To him [George Harris, the character seeking

to escape] it is the right of a man to be a man, and not a brute; the right to call the wife of his bosom his wife, and to protect her from lawless violence; the right to protect and educate his child; the right to have a home of his own, a character of his own, unsubject to the will of another.[133]

Further on Stowe writes, "O, ye who take freedom from man, with what words shall you answer it to God?"[134] Then also consider the words of Ronald Reagan:

Freedom is never more than one generation from extinction. We didn't pass it on to our children in the bloodstream. The only way they can inherit the freedom we have known is to fight for it, protect it, defend it, and then hand it to them with the well fought lessons of how they in their lifetime must do the same. And if you and I don't do this, then you and I may well spend our sunset years telling our children and their children what it was once like to live in America when men were free.[135]

My, how we have lost that sense of longing for not just freedom but for liberty. The idea of freedom now is often twisted into claiming rights beyond those that are God given and contribute toward the pursuit of happiness. The framers of the Constitution recognized this, because if you say these rights are derived and granted by men, then men can take them away. Often the so called rights today are demanded, selfish, and detrimental to the individual and society.

You know the "rights" I am referring to. They would include the purported right to abortion, the "rights" of LGBTQ+, and the growing list added to that. Why can't we admit that what is happening is the undermining of parental authority, the destruction of the family, and the unraveling of what constitutes a healthy, thriving community and nation?

The moral fabric of our nation is one of the areas our enemies love to see lowered because it shows us as weak. How is it that in the pursuit of having so called "rights" our God-given rights are potentially taken away? As individuals speak out or take a stand for traditional values, (pro-life, biblical marriage, two genders) that speech gets labeled hate speech, and they are censored or canceled, they essentially lose the right to free speech. If the demand for your "right" causes another to lose their rights, is yours legitimate?

The idea behind freedom doesn't mean across-the-board equality in the socialist sense. Freedom is like a bridge crossed to equality, but once on the other side we have to allow for individual responsibility, merit, personal differences, and human nature to play out. Therefore, it is impossible to have equality of outcomes. In the desire for liberty and a representative form of government, it is easy to see that, from our list given in the previous chapter, much of what is going on with the size of government, the leanings of the government, and the goals of certain agencies falls contrary to what our founders envisioned. What do groups like the WEF with their "Great Reset" have in mind for not only America but for the world? What are their goals in using DEI under the guise of caring about people and the planet?

One goal that has been cited is explained by Carol Roth in her book *You Will Own Nothing; Your War with a New Financial World Order and How You Can Fight Back*. Roth cites an article published in 2016 in which the WEF says, "The number one prediction was, 'You'll own nothing, and you'll be happy.'"[136]

In a way this is already true—we don't own anything . . . and if you don't believe that, just wait until you die. But obviously, that flies in the face of free market capitalism and the American dream of home ownership and property rights. So, let's suppose that the elite achieve this by 2030 and it becomes reality. I am struck by the fact that the converse would also become true: the elite would own everything . . . and be miserable.

One is reminded of the words of Mark 8:36 in the Bible, "For what does it profit a person to gain the whole world, and forfeit his soul? Those words are from Jesus, who, incidentally, was offered all the kingdoms of the world if He would but worship the devil (Matthew 4:8). That offer is now in the hearts and minds of the elites, the ones who want world domination (globalization), whether they be communists, Muslims, Catholics, the UN, or others. We know from Scripture that we will have difficult days (2 Timothy 3:1).

Remember the summer days by the Mississippi River and the swarms of mayflies I wrote about in chapter 3? That is illustrative of the time that will be given in the end to Satan and the Antichrist. The mayfly lives for but a day, and in light of eternity all that the elites and the Antichrist will gain is for a brief time; "the triumphing of the wicked will be short and the joy of the godless momentary" (Job 20:5). Another passage that comes to mind is James 5:1–8:

> Come now, you rich people, weep and howl for your miseries which are coming upon you. Your riches have rotted and your garments have become moth-eaten. Your gold and your silver have corroded, and their corrosion will serve as a testimony against you and will consume

your flesh like fire. It is in the last days that you have stored up your treasure! Behold, the pay of the laborers who mowed your fields, and which has been withheld by you, cries out against you; and the outcry of those who did the harvesting has reached the ears of the Lord of armies. You have lived for pleasure on the earth and have lived luxuriously; you have fattened your hearts in a day of slaughter. You have condemned and put to death the righteous person; he offers you no resistance. Therefore be patient, therefore, brothers and sisters, until the coming of the Lord. Behold, the farmer waits for the precious produce of the soil, being patient about it, until it gets the early and late rains. You too be patient; strengthen your hearts, for the coming of the Lord is at hand.

It is no wonder that the direction world leaders are pushing is toward oneness, new world order, and globalization. We should not be surprised or resign ourselves to saying this is a conspiracy theory. Yet it is more favorable to be labeled a conspiracy theorist than to believe the doctrines of demons (see 1 Timothy 4:1). I would label one of those doctrines as such, the one that teaches climate change along with the opinion that we need to "save the planet," making it acceptable to have people killed off to lower the population. The method used is immaterial—whether a virus or a vaccination—as long as, in their view, it is justified and means that the planet is better off for it.

Another doctrine promoted today is that the individual can change their gender. Much of that which is based on lies and deception falls under the category of demonic teaching. As Christians, we know that "the whole world lies in the power of the evil one" (1 John 5:19). Satan will use the ideas, world leaders, governments, institutions, churches, agencies, and causes to bring things to his desired end.

Don't misinterpret that to mean that I think every single individual is on board with Satan. I am thankful for God's truth that, as Christians, we have "overcome the world." Many of the elites who think they are the experts and can become "gods" have been deceived by Satan. Then again, all who are without Christ are deceived and blinded: "even if our gospel is veiled, it is veiled to those who are perishing, in whose case the god of this world has blinded the minds of the unbelieving so that they will not see the light of the gospel of the glory of Christ, who is the image of God" (2 Corinthians 4:3–4).

Now is a good time to remind ourselves of what the gospel is. Simply put, one is born again by believing and trusting in the finished work of Christ. The apostle Paul laid this out clearly in 1 Corinthians 15:1–5:

> Now I make known to you, brothers and sisters, the gospel which I preached to you, which also you received, in which you also stand, by which you also are saved, if you hold firmly to the word I preached to you, unless you believed in vain, For I handed down to you as of first importance what I also received, that Christ died for our sins according to the Scriptures, and that He was buried, and that He was raised on the third day according to the Scriptures.

Paul writes of other times Christ appeared. In 2 Corinthians 3:17 he identifies one of the benefits the Christian has received as a result of the salvation Christ has afforded: liberty: "Where the Spirit of the Lord is, there is liberty." He was not writing about political, earthly liberty. We have this promised liberty regardless of the government we are under or the nation we live in. The word "liberty" is included on our list in the previous chapter. To repeat, it means the quality or state of being free; the power to do as one pleases; freedom from physical restraint; freedom from arbitrary or despotic control; and the positive enjoyment of various social and economic rights and privileges.[137] I might add that this isn't freedom to do whatever we want but what we ought.

CHAPTER 8

FACING ISSUES

Before moving on to the subject of citizenship, I asked myself, "What are some of the social factors that indicate we need change in our country?" These factors are symptoms that deal with us as individuals—things for which we as citizens can take personal responsibility and which prospective citizens can consider carefully before taking an informed place in society. Again, this nation will never become what we are capable of being until we deal with our own lives on a personal level. We have all had struggles with sin, and some continue in sin while others recognize the need to humbly admit that we cannot change by our own strength. We need the power of the gospel and its truth, and we see our need for dependence on God by the power of the Holy Spirit to live in His truth, forgiveness, and freedom.

These issues we will highlight reflect some of the ways in which we have experienced a downward spiral in terms of the social fabric of our communities and nation. Yet more important than facing these issues is coming to terms with the truth of what was covered at the end of chapter 7—the gospel. Facing the reality of who Jesus is and what He has done has eternal significance that goes infinitely beyond the way we function as citizens in society.

Abortion: This is a subject that has already been touched upon in chapter 2. I mentioned there that this is an emotional issue for many. Despite whether someone is pro-choice or pro-life, this is at the political level an issue the country needs to figure out. By the way, I think it was clever of the abortion rights people to switch their lingo to saying they are pro-choice. I mean, who isn't for giving people the ability to choose, in this case while neglecting to offer the option of adoption. Now it is all about calling the pro-choice selection "reproductive freedom." Again, who doesn't want freedom and rights? The problem is that the organizations primarily offering their so-called service for the "health" of the woman push only for one choice, and that is abortion.

Could it be that many women claim to be for choice because they think that's what other women expect them to say? What pro-choice women need to realize is that, too often, what they are really saying is, "I would never have my baby killed, but it's okay for you to." As I said, this is an emotional issue. While advocating a strong pro-life position, we have to be careful of being so inflexible that we give the impression that we don't care about what women are going through. There really are situations in which the life of the mother is jeopardized, and in every instance there is a need for sensitivity, understanding, and compassion.

The abortion debate is by its very nature divisive—as divisive as was the slavery issue leading up to the Civil War. There are some notable parallels between the two. The slavery issue divided the country geographically between the North and the South. Although the abortion issue isn't a geographical division, it is becoming that way with individual states differing in allowing or restricting abortion laws.

Both sides have considered the subject of debate (the slave/ the baby) as being nonhuman. In the book *The Demon of Unrest* by Erik Larson, the events surrounding Fort Sumter and the beginning of the Civil War are chronicled. Larson wrote about a speaker who came to Charleston, South Carolina, and noted, "The city's white population was a willing audience for a series of lectures given in 1850 by Louis Agassiz, a Harvard zoologist who claimed that scientific observation proved that Blacks were inferior to whites and thus merited enslavement."[138]

Many claims like that were made during this period of our history and used as rationale for slavery, even by Christians. Today, the baby in the womb is often referred to as simply a fetus, removing the idea of human personage—unless, of course, the baby is wanted. We have come a long way in science and in understanding DNA, and we now know that we share in common about 99.9 percent of DNA with each other. The racist wants to use that other small percentage that determines melanin and the darkness of skin as a basis for racism. It is true, also, of course, that we share 99.9 percent of our DNA with a baby in the womb, regardless of the level of development.

Another parallel is that both slavery and abortion had and have similar motivation, and that is money. The slavery institution fought to maintain the level of economy the landowners were enjoying with free labor. The abortion industry is one of the biggest unregulated industries there is, and those involved, too, are motivated by money. (In 2022–23 Planned Parenthood reported $2.1 billion in income and over $2.5 billion in net assets.)[139]

"The rationale for the institution of slavery gave rise in the early 1900s to modern eugenics, the idea that race could be purified by selective breeding and the elimination of flawed people."[140] It became, not slavery and its parallel to abortion, but racism and its tie to abortion. With regard to both slavery/racism and abortion, the key question is, "What kind of attitude should we have toward human life, whatever the race, whatever the point of development? And to what extent should we value life, whatever the race, whatever the point of development?" It is said that if you devalue life at any level you devalue it at all levels. Life is sacred, and that is why the bottom line is referred to by pro-lifers as the sanctity of life.

It is important to consider the history of the abortion issue. The abortion movement was founded by Margaret Sanger, and it is telling to recognize that she was a racist who taught eugenics. In the early days of her illegal approaches to push birth control (which was like a religion to her), she faced opposition. In 1942 she was able to change the name of the organization she had begun to Planned Parenthood Federation of America.[141] Sanger's life was one of radical political leanings; dishonesty; illicit affairs; and in the end, addictions to drugs and alcohol.[142]

Today's Planned Parenthood doesn't completely discount what Sanger was like but now claims to "reckon" with her and her views.[143] Yet they go on to tell lies about her. They claim that she was a nurse, but in reality she'd had three months of training for that field. They also claim that her view of eugenics was common for her time: "In the early 20th century, eugenic ideas were popular among highly educated, privileged, and mostly-white Americans."[144]

But even if that were true, stating that certain ideas were common doesn't make them right. Bear in mind that those same ideas were taken to the limit by Germany in the 1930s. The truth is that Planned Parenthood is an organization built on lies and deception and on a person with a legacy of divorces; immorality; and in the end, alcoholism and drug abuse.[145] Planned Parenthood doesn't provide those details on their website.

It was hoped that, as a result of the Dobbs decision mentioned in chapter 2, the number of abortions in America would decrease. It may be that the reason the number of abortions hasn't gone down is because of the abortion pill called mifepristone (sold as an easy thing: "just take this "medicine"). The other methods for terminating a pregnancy are aspiration, dilation, evacuation, and induction.[146]

I would add partial-birth abortion; even though it was outlawed on November 5, 2003, it continues. "In 2021 the CDC reported a total of 625,978 abortions from 46 states and Washington, DC." If you are in the business of killing, to lie about stats will be no problem. In reality, from 1973 to 2021, 65,464,760 abortions occurred.[147] I would encourage an honest look at the history both of Sanger and of Planned Parenthood, at abortion methods, and at the development of a baby in the womb to help determine where you stand on this issue. One should also consider related topics, such as botched abortions (complications and even death of the mother), harvesting body parts, and infanticide.

The stand against being pro-choice is based on science, but also on sociopolitical and economic considerations. The founders were not thinking of abortion when they wrote the Declaration of Independence and included these words: "... that [individuals] are endowed by their Creator with certain unalienable Rights, that among these are Life, Liberty and the Pursuit of Happiness." But wouldn't those rights be extended to the unborn, provided they are persons? The economic effects of birth control and abortion, are seen when considering the shortage of people in the workforce who would otherwise be paying into the economy and into funds like Social Security.

Along with economic, social, and political aspects and science, we also have the authoritative basis from Scripture to help us in taking a stand for life. The title of the first book of the Bible, Genesis, means beginning. In the account of creation, as the first couple are created in God's image, Scripture says in Genesis 1:28: "God blessed them; and God said to them, 'Be fruitful and multiply, and fill the earth.' There are also the memorable words of David in Psalm 139:13–14: "You created my innermost parts; you wove me in my mother's womb. I will give thanks to You, because I am awesomely and wonderfully made; wonderful are Your works, and my soul knows it very well."

Consider also the account of Mary and Elizabeth in Luke 1:41–44. When Elizabeth hears Mary's voice (both women being pregnant), she exclaims to Mary that her baby "leaped in my womb for joy." The emotion of joy very much indicates personhood.

A developing but unborn human baby deserves a continuation of the life with which it has already been gifted. In the discussion of "When does life begin?" I have heard it said that the answer is based on brain activity. Others assert that it is determined by viability—the ability to live, grow, and develop. Well, that is already true at the moment of conception.

It is interesting to note that, since abortion was legalized, the technology and ability to keep premature babies alive at earlier and earlier points of development has steadily improved. I believe that the biblical answer to the above question is when there is blood; this is based on Leviticus 17:11, which states that "the life of the flesh is in the blood." Not only is there blood from very early on, but the heart and blood vessels develop already at about 16 days after fertilization. The shedding of that blood through the act of abortion would be classified scripturally, then, as the taking of a life. The Bible, as in Exodus 20:13, would call abortion murder.

I have included more content on this issue than on the ones to follow; that is because I believe our stance on this issue is vital to where we are as a nation and people. Within the Dobbs decision we have been encouraged on a state level to engage in discussion and debate in the public square. Consider this my contribution to the debate.

Alcoholism: It doesn't take much to see the prevalence of the use and abuse of alcohol in our country. One can rarely gather at holidays; sporting events, both college and pro; receptions; and neighborhood parties without alcohol being consumed. We see this as a problem when it is excessive (defined as five or more drinks for a man and four or more for a woman on a single occasion).[148] Overall, 62 percent of US adults say that they drink alcohol,[149] and the statistics show that Americans are imbibing as much liquor per capita as they did during the Civil War. Apparently, the increase we see today is due to women drinking almost as much as men.

Susan Stewart, a sociologist and demographer at Iowa State University, notes that "wines are marketed to women: the fancy labels with flowers on them and the pretty colors." Stewart tracks "a normalization of alcohol in our daily lives" that is encouraging women and men to drink. "It's infiltrated our daily activities that didn't typically involve alcohol, like sporting events, or a 5K; there is a beer tent at the end."[150] It cannot be refuted that alcohol has been the source of much societal turmoil in areas like underage drinking, binge drinking, drunk driving, and more.

Debt: personal and national—Americans currently carry record high amounts of household debt. "For the year (Q3 2024) US household debt reached a record high of 17.94 trillion, according to data from the Federal Reserve Bank of New York."[151] The area with the largest increase in any category (categories include mortgage, home equity, auto loan, and student loan) was credit card debt. "Mortgage debt is most Americans' largest debt, exceeding other types by a wide margin. Student loans are the next-largest type of debt among those listed in the data, followed closely by auto loans."[152] There are reports that inflation has eased, and the cool down could be due to 2024 having been an election year. We would be hard pressed to find Americans who haven't seen budgets stretched while the cost of living has gone up.

Our national debt is now over thirty-six trillion dollars. The causes for our debt vary, but, simply put, we spend more than we take in. When government refuses to work with a balanced budget, it has to borrow to make up the difference, resulting in a deficit, which adds to the incomprehensible total of our nation's debt. "Our deficits are caused by predictable structural factors: our aging baby-boomer generation, rising healthcare cost, and a tax system that does not bring in enough to pay for what the government promised its citizens."[153] It is said that America has been in debt since its beginning and that this is simply a fact of life.

Should we care about household and national debt? The obvious answer is yes. According to Proverbs 22:7, "The rich rules over the poor, and the borrower becomes the lender's slave." The national debt is insurmountable, which means that it is impossible to gain control of it, and it will take generations to pay. We are on an unsustainable path to financial ruin and bankruptcy—if not that, the situation will require at least a major debt restructure.

Divorce: It is grievous to consider divorce in America because so many people have been affected by it. There was a time when my own marriage was on the brink of becoming a statistic, and we all know people who have experienced divorce, either directly or in terms of parents who have gone through it.

The list of statistics on divorce is lengthy. Here are some: The divorce rate has [thankfully!] been falling in recent years, and it hit a record low in 2019.[154] The average length of marriage prior to divorce is eight years. Couples who live together before marriage increase their likelihood of divorce by 40 percent, and having friends who have divorced increases the risk for themselves to 75 percent. Of divorced couples, 60 percent cite infidelity as a reason.[155]

One could go on and look at rates, the cost of divorce, and detail of the trends, but, put simply, the divorce rate is a major indicator affecting the social strength of America. In 1969 no-fault divorce first became legal, and by 2010 it had been made legal in every state. It is easy to see how the issue of divorce has been a blight on our country. I would encourage those of you who have faced it or who feel threatened by it now to seek help. Get counseling, hang in there, and stay committed to one another. There is hope.

Education: Education is another area in which we see downward trends.[156] Secular humanism, critical race theory, sex education, multiculturalism, gender ideology, and relativism rule the day in much of the teaching. Children are no longer taught civics and how to value the history, uniqueness, and strengths of America. Add to this other ideas to which students are being exposed, often in a negative way: transgenderism, diversity, equity, inclusion (DEI), social justice, identity politics, the teaching that America is a racist nation, etc.

Gambling: Iowa is one of a handful of states that offer every form of gambling that is available. There would be more states on that list, but some don't have a Native American tribe that can offer tribal gambling.[157] In 1989 Iowa became the fourth state to adopt non-Native American commercial casino gambling and the first to introduce riverboat gambling. In 1990 the Dubuque Racing Association was the first applicant approved to operate a river gambling boat in the state.[158]

My guess is that Dubuque offers more forms of gambling than even Las Vegas: riverboat, casino, dog track, lottery, as well as online sports gambling. At the time of this writing, there are over thirty online sports books. Not every state allows sports betting, but thirty-eight do.[159] The economic impact of gambling is $329 billion annually.[160]

Whenever commercials for gambling are aired, the advertisers are required to provide the 800 number for help for those for whom gambling has become an addiction. About 1.2–6.2 percent of Americans have a gambling problem, meaning that as many as 20 million are problem gamblers.[161]

Since gambling is now more accessible with online betting, the age group that has more addicts than any other is 18–24, at 7.1 percent.[162] Young people are more susceptible to the dopamine and endorphin rush gambling generates because their brains are still developing, and thus they more easily become addicted. For all ages there is the trade-off of short-term pleasure for long-term consumption or wealth. It seems that watching sports for the entertainment value isn't enough—to the point that the appreciation of the sport for many hinges primarily on how their bets have faired. George Orwell in his book *1984* wrote, "Heavy physical work, the care of home and children, petty quarrels with neighbors, films, football, beer, and above all, gambling filled up the horizon of their minds. To keep them in control was not difficult."[163]

The call may come for more regulation, but the damage is already being done. With legislation, social acceptance, and availability, gambling is no longer seen as a vice. There are plenty of reasons to stand against gambling, however. No goods or services are provided. It is like a voluntary tax, when we already pay too much. It can lead to corruption, addiction, violence, crime, family neglect (due to expenditure not only of money but also of time), and even suicide.

The gambling issue is like the debt issue, as both bring about a disregard for their effect on future generations. We need to ask ourselves, "What is this teaching the next generation?" Do we want them to live with an ongoing obsession with money without experiencing the value of hard work?

Open borders and illegal immigration: I am all for immigration and people coming to America for a better life, as many of our ancestors did, legally. They came, assimilated, and succeeded as Americans. The problem is that, with the large number coming in who are unvetted, there are undoubtedly those who are here as criminals and enemies. Such is the case with the gang members from Venezuela called Tren de Aragua.[164]

It is said that there are between 11 and 12 million unauthorized immigrants living in the US. To put this in context, in 2022 there were a total of 46.2 million immigrants living in the US, more than three-quarters of whom were here legally.[165] In the areas in which many unauthorized immigrants have ended up, resources are being exhausted. It is unsustainable to continue this way. Then, also, there are the increases in crime and in the distribution of fentanyl.[166]

Is it possible that, due to irresponsible and unconstitutional actions on the part of government and the outright violation of law, America as a nation could lose its uniqueness? There is a reason our nation adopted a national motto of *e pluribus unum*— "Out of many, one." Will the many (including those among the illegal immigrants who come with bad intentions) and the rest of us truly want to be "one"? Such unity means knowing and understanding what the ideas and ideals, values and beliefs are that have made us unique in America. It means citizenship.

Pornography: Pornography is similar to gambling in that both are addictions, and both have been made readily accessible online. Porn, gambling, and alcoholism also share in common an invisible line that, once crossed, means that the individual no longer has the control they once thought they had.

Men are more likely to be involved in watching pornography than women because men tend to be more visual in the area of objectifying women. However, many women objectify men as well. "Approximately 69 percent of American men and 40 percent of women view online porn each year."[167] "Men in their 30's and 40's report the most use of pornography."[168] And many young adults admit that they have viewed pornography at some point in their lives. The negative effects of pornography are numerous. Men who are given over to it tend to more often feel lonely, insecure, and dissatisfied with their physical appearance.

This issue ties into the divorce problem as well, because "56% of American divorces involve one party having an 'obsessive interest' in pornographic websites."[169] There are ways to get help and to attain freedom from pornographic enslavement.

On a personal level, pornography was introduced into my life at a young age. This is in no way unique, based as it is on natural curiosity. But even as a relatively new Christian and an individual young in marriage, I had periodic struggles with pornography. I got to the point at which I needed to make a serious decision against allowing this to be a part of my life. I made a vow before the Lord that I would never purposely pursue viewing pornography, and by the grace of God I have kept that vow. A related problem in today's culture is that many movie scenes are becoming more openly pornographic. TV and movies could as a topic be added to this list, along with music, as they are all further indicators of where we are both as individuals and as a nation.

In summary, we have looked briefly at a variety of issues that are affecting us as a society. There are many ways in which we could describe the "state of the union." We are facing moral decline, decay, social dysfunction, institutional failure, unraveling of the family, loss of freedoms, decline of work ethic, apathy, disunity, polarization, and cynicism. Does all of this mean that we should resort to ultimate pessimism? I don't think we have to give up hope, though these realities are sobering. I have hope because there is always opportunity for change. People and nations have changed when they have experienced revival and a call to repentance. The great thing about that is we don't have to look to leaders and government for that possibility.

CHAPTER 9

IMMIGRATION AND CITIZENSHIP

Before the founding colonists were citizens of a new country, they were British subjects. The founders pledged their "lives, fortunes, and sacred honor"[170] to gain a new citizenship, without knowing for sure what that would look like. They established a government brought about by men meeting secretly and drafting the Constitution in the summer of 1787.

The idea of citizenship goes back hundreds of years. The Greeks and Romans placed a high value on citizenship. Aspects of being a citizen included land ownership, participating in politics, having protection, and involvement in military service. Peter J. Spiro, in *Citizenship: What Everyone Needs to Know*, writes about two types of citizenship at birth: *jus soli*—"right of the soil"—and *jus sanguines*—"right of the blood."[171] The former has to do with where you are born and the latter with who you were born to—your ancestry.

Spiro goes on to write: "Absolute territorial birthright citizenship has its roots in the feudal era. Under medieval conceptions of natural order, individuals were born into the protections of sovereigns, to whom they owed perpetual allegiance in return."[172] The feudal era is a reference to the Middle Ages in Europe. This was a social and political system involving landowners and the tenants who worked on their parcels of land.[173]

Throughout the history of America we have experienced challenges, changes, and ongoing debate regarding immigration and citizenship. An example: before the Civil War in 1857, the Supreme Court in the Dred Scott decision ruled that a person of African descent could not hold national citizenship, even if they were free.[174] That all changed through war and the Constitutional amendment under Lincoln which states that "all persons born in the United States, and subject to the Jurisdiction thereof, are citizens of the United States and of the State wherein they reside."[175] That amendment has been and is now part of the ongoing debate about automatic birthright citizenship.

Although we won't delve too deeply into birthright citizenship, it is something to be concerned about. Many think that the 14th Amendment's intent was not to grant blanket, universal citizenship to everyone born within the United States. If birthright citizenship gets taken away, how will that affect those who, though born here, are no longer deemed a citizen or who have at least one parent who is here illegally? My own son-in-law was born in the Philippines to an American father and a Filipino mother who doesn't have US citizenship, but she is in the US legally with permanent residency. There are no easy answers for the many scenarios surrounding citizenship and non-citizenship. We also don't want to create unnecessary fear of deportation.

The Indian Citizenship Act of 1924, by which Native Americans were extended birth citizenship, is another example.[176] Both of the instances cited above involved people who already resided in the US. We are, after all, a nation of immigrants. Many from Europe became naturalized and gave up their previous nationality. In most cases they transferred their loyalty to their new country, as mentioned in chapter 2.

The US Immigration and Nationality Act of 1952 brought changes. "It ended Asian exclusion from immigrating to the US and introduced a system of preferences based on skill sets and family reunification."[177] This act became law in the midst of the Cold War, and there was concern for national security. The idea that the United States "could face communist infiltration through immigration and that unassimilated aliens could threaten the foundations of American life"[178] appears to be altogether forgotten today. Yet it can still be said that "the United States has a long, disgraceful history of racial qualifications for naturalization extending well into the modern era."[179]

GOVERNMENT AGENCIES FOR IMMIGRATION

When our ancestors immigrated, the process of attaining citizenship was straightforward, especially for those going through legal channels. The system under which we now operate is a confusing process. There are many agencies involved, and the steps are very complex. The agencies involved are the Department of State, Immigration and Customs Enforcement (ICE), United States Citizenship and Immigration Services (USCIS), and the Department of Homeland Security. The US Department of State issues visas. Immigration and Customs Enforcement has an investigative role and enforces immigration laws. ICE also has the task of detaining and removing undocumented aliens, and USCIS oversees those who seek lawful entry into the US They conduct a naturalization interview, give English and civics tests, and conduct green card interviews. The Department of

Homeland Security (DHS) is like an umbrella over USCIS, US Customs and Border Protection, and ICE.[180]

It is often said that, if the laws regarding immigration were enforced, we wouldn't be having as great of a problem at the borders. That makes it sound as if these agencies are choosing not to do their job, when actually they have not always been allowed to do it. The Customs and Border Protection Agency (CBP) is the "nation's largest federal law enforcement agency charged with securing the nation's borders and facilitating international travel and trade, which prevent people from entering the country illegally and bringing anything harmful or illegal into the United States."[181]

President Biden pledged in 2020 that his policies would allow for an open border,[182] but those policies have led to crises and have helped migrants to illegally enter the country with impunity. We now have an estimated 11–12 million unauthorized immigrants,[183] as has been stated earlier. The countries of origin vary—two-thirds of the migrants are from Mexico and Central America, but the remaining statistics are as follows: about 1.2 million are from Asia; close to 1.1 million from South America; 780,000 from Europe, Canada, or Oceania; 436,000 from the Caribbean; and 321,000 from Africa.[184] In 2022 the total population of those who were foreign born reached 46.2 million in the United States, as was also mentioned previously.[185]

The terms used for those coming vary as well. The "migrant" could be called undocumented, unauthorized, or illegal. In my view the term "illegal immigrant" seems to fit best since coming into the country illegally became their first act upon arrival to the US.

Most Americans favor immigrants coming to America. The inspiring words of Emma Lazarus from the poem she wrote to help raise money for the pedestal for the Statue of Liberty are well known: "Give me your tired, your poor, your huddled masses yearning to breathe free, the wretched refuse of your teeming shore. Send these, the homeless, tempest-tossed to me, I lift my lamp beside the golden door!"[186] These words are an invitation to those who come for opportunity, freedom, and the hope of a better life.

America proudly became what has been referred to as a melting pot. The concern we now have is due not only to the numbers of immigrants but to the percentage of them who may be criminals, enemies, and terrorists who may seek to destroy America.[187] There is the gang from Venezuela that was already mentioned, but also drug cartels, human traffickers (sex trade and child labor), and distributors of fentanyl. The estimated deaths from fentanyl in 2023 was approximately 72,000, with an average of 200 happening per day.[188]

China, as we know, is behind the production of fentanyl. Peter Schweizer, in *Blood Money: Why the Powerful Turn a Blind Eye While China Kills Americans*, relates the history of China's production and distribution of the drug: "Clearly, China was weaponizing fentanyl against the United States, However, quantities were limited by parcel services. Then a solution emerged; instead of shipping fentanyl incrementally through the mail, why not mass-produce it in Mexico?"[189] It is in light of this that drug cartels factor in and that smuggling across the border takes place.

Included in Schweizer's writing are other aspects of the way China is undermining the strength of the US. Of concern is the number of Chinese nationals who are being encountered at the border: "So far in FY24, 24,376 Chinese nationals have been encountered at the Southwest border. Encounters of Chinese nationals in March of 2024 increased 8,500 percent compared to March 2021, and have surpassed all of last fiscal year—just 6 months into FY24."[190] There is no reason to think that Chinese immigrants are all here to create problems; to be sure, many have fled China and rightly claim asylum. The same could be said, of course, of any immigrant group, including those asylum-seeking migrants who have flooded in from our own hemisphere.

Lest one think that the potential threat is from only a couple of countries, I hasten to add that there are others. There are those called "inadmissible aliens" and others called "significant-interest aliens."[191] The designation "inadmissible" applies to someone barred from entering the country because of a health concern or due to their carrying fraudulent documents. Significant-interest aliens are individuals with known ties to terrorism. It was reported by Chief Border Patrol agent Aaron Heitke from San Diego, as he swore under oath to the Homeland Security Committee, that there has been an increase since 2021 in arrests made of significant-interest aliens. He was told to keep quiet about those totals because "the administration was trying to convince the public that there was no threat at the border."[192]

Besides China, the other countries being mentioned in reports are Ukraine, Venezuela, Cuba, Haiti, and Nicaragua. As a matter of fact, however, individuals with terrorism ties are coming from several different countries.[193] It is difficult to not get overwhelmed by our current conditions of immigration. There is urgent need to gain some clarity of the process and terms.

Who Gets In?

In 2023 *The New York Times* offered a rundown on the process for immigrants in an article titled "Who Gets In? A Guide to America's Chaotic Border Rules."[194] In summary, it goes like this—migrants wanting to cross the border can seek humanitarian parole, get an appointment at a border checkpoint, or proceed to cross illegally. Once across, they can be detained and deported or get a temporary release into the US, if they have not already moved on and evaded detection.

The difference between a refugee and an asylum seeker is based on present location. A refugee is still outside the country, but an asylum-seeker is present in the country and submits an application. Once granted asylum, such persons become asylees. The asylum request receives a response that is either affirmative or defensive, based on the person's circumstances. Affirmative responses are given to those who are not in removal proceedings and who have filed within one year of US arrival.

The defensive asylum process is for those who are here without authorization or who have been placed in removal proceedings in immigration court.[195] Asylum is a legal status obtained when it can be shown that the individual would face persecution (for race, religion, nationality, membership in a particular group, or political opinion) or other risk at home. The risk faced, along with persecution, could be due to poverty, political unrest, a natural disaster, or gang violence.[196]

The Immigration Act of 1990 allowed for a designation of Temporary Protected Status (TPS). Designated countries with some of these already listed conditions give foreign nationals a work permit and protection from deportation. "The Secretary of Homeland Security has discretion to decide when a country merits TPS designation."[197] An individual who is eligible submits an application to USCIS and is given temporary protection from deportation, along with temporary authorization to work in the US TPS doesn't provide a path to lawful permanent residence (green card) or citizenship.[198]

TERMS SURROUNDING IMMIGRATION

It is easy to confuse some of the terminology surrounding immigration, and the relevant words are often used interchangeably. A review of some of the basic terms follows in this paragraph. To be an *emigrant* refers to a person's relationship with the country from which they are moving. The term *immigrant*, on the other hand, refers to that person's status in the country they move to. One becomes a *refugee* because of a situation in which they now seek refuge in another country. The word *asylum* applies when one seeks international protection but has not been approved for refugee status. Humanitarian parole allows one who may be deemed inadmissible to be in the US for a temporary period—that is the TPS designation.

If someone has done something that helped the US government, they can be granted a Special Immigrant Visa (SIV). An example of this is translators/interpreters for the military in Iraq or Afghanistan. This kind of visa is applied for with USCIS as a path to a green card. Some migrants are those who have moved, not because of threat or persecution but to improve their lives by finding work, attaining a better education, or reuniting with family.[199] With humanitarian parole there is a per month limit of 30,000. There is also the possibility that a migrant might gain a sponsor in the US who will provide financial help. If an application is approved, the person must have lived in the US for at least two years. For this to work "they need a valid passport and money to pay for a plane ticket."[200]

The immigrant entering via the US Southern border can use an app called CBPOne, which can be used to arrange an asylum appointment, but they have to be near the border at the time of application, and the process is subject to glitches. There are about one thousand such appointments available per day. (This app has, since the time of writing, been canceled under the new administration in 2025.)

If an appointment is made, the individual is probably released into the US. They can apply for asylum but may wait months or years for a court date. If that doesn't work for them, they are turned away. There are the thousands who cross illegally, which can be dangerous but in some areas is not necessarily difficult. "People who enter the country without proper documentation will either be put into formal deportation proceedings, which is a years-long, drawn out process, or an expedited removal process that is intended to process and deport people much faster."[201] From a processing center many are released within the US for a future court date that, again, can take months or years.

Others can be sent on their way to deportation and a felony charge, especially if they were not fleeing persecution or danger. If the conditions that warrant asylum don't exist, they will probably be deported. Migrants now have to document that they have applied for asylum in Mexico or in any other country they have passed through. Many are coached on what to say to gain asylum. There has to be a credible claim that they have faced persecution at home. If released into the country, they will still have to show denial of asylum by the countries they passed through whenever they do go to court.[202]

Many asylum claims can take years to work through the system and still be denied. The "got-aways" who have circumvented the system and made it in could be anywhere, and they live with the risk and uncertainty of possible discovery and deportation. With all the problems at the border, there is also the possibility of "catch and release." "Catch and Release" refers to releasing migrants into the US while they await hearings. This policy is encouraging more and more to come, and it makes the cartels more inclined and emboldened to increase their activities of drug and human smuggling.[203] When the totals of the incoming are more than one million annually, it is impossible to vet those coming in who might be a threat to security.

There is an aspect of the agencies and system we have in place that has led to misconduct and abuse by CBP and ICE. For an understanding of some of what has been known to occur, the book *Illegal: How America's Immigration Regime Threatens Us All* by Elizabeth Cohen is informative. She writes,

> Whatever one thinks about unauthorized immigration, a system that fails to ensure basic due process for people ensnared in immigration courts or deportation proceedings is a system grossly indifferent to a foundational principle of any democratic country. We already know that some people in deportation proceedings are US citizens. Some get deported. Many mistakes are made, people's fundamental rights are denied, and the wrong people get deported because ICE so often is exempt from even basic judicial oversight.[204]

Cohen reminds us throughout her book that, if we care about immigration and the realities of deportation, we should be careful to avoid racist, nativist, White supremacy, and White nationalist attitudes that tend to motivate policy and process.

Much of the present immigration process is tedious and convoluted, and I hope I haven't lost you somewhere along the way. That said, please bear with me, as there are just a few more aspects I want to touch on in relation to immigration. These will only be brief mentions. First, there is the potential of a future granting of amnesty to all of the illegal immigrants residing in the country. To grant amnesty means to pardon those who have committed a crime or offense.

Of course, this would be an admission that these individuals are here illegally. In a way many are already being given what is called a "quiet amnesty." This is due to the many cases that, though completed, have not been adjudicated by the Justice's Executive Office for Immigration Review, the point at which they are dismissed, terminated, or administratively closed, allowing the individuals to remain in the country without deportation.[205] A second and opposite possibility would be massive numbers of deportations. How that would be handled and the cost involved would be of major concern.

Also of concern is the potential effect of illegal immigration on voter fraud. What would it mean for non-citizens to be allowed to vote? There are situations in which immigrants are treated better than some of our own, like veterans, with the intention that they would feel obligated to vote favorably for the Left since they are the ones who have provided the open door.

The idea of using immigration to increase election votes is nothing new. Spiro writes, "In the US immigrants were naturalized mostly by state court judges until 1906. The process was exploited by urban political machines to pad electoral rolls with new voters. Congress responded with legislation giving federal courts exclusive jurisdiction over naturalization."[206]

NATURALIZATION PROCESS

Good citizenship begins with the desire to be a citizen. The process in the direction of citizenship is called naturalization, and it grants the same rights and responsibilities to the naturalized citizen as to those who are born here. Application is made, a test given, and the final step is an oath-taking ceremony. The cost can range from $380.00–$760.00, or $710.00 if filing online. The application form is N-400, and it is filed with USCIS. The lower amount of $380.00 applies if the applicant qualifies for a reduced fee based on annual household income. The time involved is 18–24 months. The applicant has to be 18 years old and has to have been a resident for at least five years (or three years if married to a US citizen) and meet all the other requirements.[207] There is more involved, like a biometrics appointment and an interview. For information on all of this, go to USCIS.gov. Appendix A at the end of this book provides a resource listing of websites and phone numbers.

CITIZENSHIP PROCESS

With the mention of naturalization, it is now time to move on to the subject of citizenship. It is easy to assume, as I did, that all it takes is for unauthorized immigrants to sign up for citizenship. But "naturalization is predicated on legal permanent residence, which in turn is subject to various threshold qualifications relating to family ties, professional skills, refugee status, or other criteria."[208]

One would think that citizenship would be the desire of the majority of those coming to the US, but that doesn't seem to be the emphasis. The indifference toward citizenship is well documented in *The Dying Citizen: How Progressive Elites, Tribalism, and Globalism Are Destroying the Idea of America* by Victor Davis Hanson. Hanson writes,

The keys to American patriotism I think are two, now vanishing, values: first, gratitude for being a citizen of the United States; second, recognition, that one immigrates to the United States or continues to live within its confines because one believes it is preferable to other countries. These truths are grounded in the reality that America's uniqueness at its birth in 1776, and throughout its various constitutional reforms and amendments, has logically made it the envied destination of most of the world's immigrants.[209]

Hanson shares a number of ways in which the importance of citizenship has been diminished and how that is affecting our country. We have covered that sufficiently. I personally encourage citizenship and appreciate that he also states that "citizen differs from visitors, aliens, and residents passing through who are not rooted inside borders where a constitution and its laws reign supreme. For citizenship to work, the vast majority of residents must be citizens. But to become citizens, residents must be invited on the condition of giving up past loyalties for those of their new host."[210] Citizenship is what makes a republic; monarchies can get along without it. What keeps a republic on its legs is good citizenship.[211]

PERSONAL EXAMPLES OF CITIZENSHIP

Following are a few examples of individuals in my own life who have had interesting experiences with citizenship. The first are friends who became burdened for missions. Russ and Cathy were led to Australia for ministry in 2006, and as of 2020 they are now dual citizens of the US and Australia. Since their children were under 18 at the time of their move, they too, have dual citizenship.

Russ works as a team member of City Bible Forum, Third Space, and ABWE (Association of Baptists for World Evangelism) in Sydney, Australia. He also manages a ministry called Reel Dialogue and writes film reviews with a desire to use movies as an inroad to create dialogue with biblical themes. The cost for citizenship at the time of their move was $285.00, but the standard fee is now $560.00. They had to be sponsored by their employer (ABWE), go through an interview, take a test, and participate in a swearing-in ceremony.

Russ and Cathy felt that citizenship demonstrated their commitment to being in Australia. It is not common for Americans to emigrate to Australia, but there are some benefits: the dual citizenship makes travel easier, they have access to national healthcare, and there are tax benefits. Russ says, "Becoming a citizen of Australia doesn't give you the accent," but he is fine that their lack of a Australian accent makes them stand out as different from other citizens (this based on personal communication with Russ).

Dual citizenship used to be looked upon as a double allegiance, and, given the analogy of bigamy, there are times when it makes sense. Even Mexico changed its law in 1998 to allow Mexicans to keep their citizenship when they naturalize in the US and elsewhere. Prior to 1998 it was an automatic policy to be terminated as a citizen there.[212]

A second personal example is that of a family member from my wife's side. I was not given permission to use their name and will respect that. My brother-in-law married a lady who was originally from the western African nation of the Republic of Ghana, and together the couple moved to the United Kingdom.

My sister-in-law is a citizen of the UK and is a doctor of anesthesiology there. She had spent nine years in Hong Kong before she and my brother-in-law met, working in a British colony hospital. (Hong Kong was a British colony from 1841 until 1997, with the exception of a period of Japanese occupation from 1941–

1945). My brother-in-law made the decision to become a dual citizen. The cost was 1,630 pounds, which is $1783.28 in USD.

To become a UK citizen one has to have lived there for five years and must pass a "Life in the UK" test, prove an understanding of English, be of "good character" (meaning that they haven't recently broken the law or declared bankruptcy), and give the names of two people who can verify their identity (these are called "referees"). The condition of having lived in the UK for up to five years is called a settled status and is also known as "indefinite leave to remain."[213]

The final example is from a cousin's grandparents, Yanatan Yossip (changed to John Joseph) and his wife, Anna, who immigrated to the United States from Persia (now Iran). John and Anna were both from towns in northern Iran—John from Ourmiah and Anna from Tabriz. John, an orphan who had been raised by Presbyterian missionaries, was a goat-herder and later a copper pot salesman. The towns they were from are a couple of hours apart, and no story passed down as to how they met. They married at a fairly young age on June 19, 1919, when John was 19 and Anna 18, toward the end of what had been terrible days for Persia.

Persia was neutral during WWI, but the result of a series of military conflicts between the Ottoman, British, and Russian Empires was the deaths of over two million Persian civilians who died due to Armenian genocide by the Ottoman regime and Persian famine. There are statistics indicating that eight to ten million people died of starvation and disease, but I have also seen figures of eighteen to twenty million.

This latter famine occurred during the span of 1917–1919; the Armenian genocide, which resulted in the annihilation of

Armenian Christians, had taken place from the spring 1915 to autumn 1916. Whatever the totals, the genocide was an act of mass atrocity. There are those who state that "about one-quarter of the population of northern Iran were killed."[214] On June 8 of 1918 an army of the Ottoman Empire entered Tabriz. By September they had gained control of the north from Tabriz to the southern shores of the Caspian Sea.[215] The area of Tabiz is where John and Anna had lived before deciding to leave.

I view their departure as an incredible venture of determination to get out of that part of the world with so much hardship around them. Think of all that went on: there was the occupation of three empires, whose presences contributed to famine (if anyone got food, it tended to be the soldiers). There had been a series of droughts, along with disease, such as the 1918 flu epidemic, and other plagues like cholera and typhus. The famine caused desperation to the point of cannibalism.

In an article written by Dr. Pat Walsh titled "Who Remembers the Persians?" the author quotes Dr. Mohammed Gholi Majd:

> The great famine of 1917–1919 was unquestionably the greatest calamity in the history of Persia, far surpassing anything that has happened before. It is shown in this study that as much as 40 percent of the population was wiped out because of starvation and the associated diseases that accompany malnutrition.[216]
>
> Unquestionably, Persia was the greatest victim of WWI. No other country had suffered casualties of this magnitude in both absolute and relative terms. Yet the greatest famine in Persia, one of the greatest famines of modern times, and definitely one of the largest genocides

of the 20th century has remained unknown and unexplored. . . . Unquestionably, the most remarkable fact about the Persian holocaust is that it has remained concealed all these years, a fact about which volumes can be written.[217]

The reason all this was concealed was that much about the famine and genocide was due to the occupation and policies of Britain. Dr. Majd describes in his book the events that took place as a result of British occupation and control. Many became refugees, my aunt's family among them.

John and Anna made their way from northern Iran, traveling at night and hiding during the day. I assume that they traveled with others, or at least with a guide. They made their way to Naples, Italy. Sailing from Naples on November 10, 1921, on the *SS Gul Djemal*, they landed in New York on December 24 of that year. This was actually their second trip; at the end of the first trip the US had set a quota, that number had been met, and they had been turned away. The United States then changed the quota, and they made the second trip.

While on that second voyage Anna had lost a baby, perhaps during childbirth. Having to spend so much time traveling would have allowed them to become familiar with the ship. I thought I would learn a bit about it, too. The *SS Gul Djemal* had a record career of seventy-five years of service (1875–1950). During that time she had various owners and names: *Germanic, Ottawa, Gul Djemal,* and *Gulcemal*. She had been built by the White Star Line, of which many are familiar because of the *Titanic*.

In 1899, while the ship was in New York, she took on water because of a severe blizzard and became top-heavy. The damage caused was not beyond repair, and in 1910 the ship was purchased by Turkey and used as a transport. The Turks and Germans were allies. "But one of the most terrible sea disasters in history occurred on May 3 1915 when the Gul Djemal was torpedoed and sunk down to the superstructure . . . she was carrying more than 4,000 troops, of which the majority was lost to the waves."[218] Other articles indicate that the ship had 1,600 soldiers. Fortunately, it didn't sink completely but was raised and again repaired.[219]

After the war the *Gul Djemal* became part of the Ottoman American Line to bring emigrants to America. On one of those trips, prior to John and Anna's, the *New York Times* reported on November 3, 1920 that "Captain Hussein Lufti, the commander, and the Turkish officers of the Gul Djemal have had a hard time with the steerage passengers, who were mostly Greeks, Armenians, Rumanians, and Bulgarians and had joined together in their hatred of the Turks."[220]

"Rumanians" is probably a misspelling of Romanians. I imagine that there may have been a bit of that same kind of contention the next year when John and Anna traveled, since the Turks had been part of the reason they left Persia. As a matter of fact, there is a short list of passengers who were not allowed to disembark right away, and John and Anna were on that list, titled, "Aliens held for special inquiry." This is speculation, but that may have been due to the loss of their baby. My cousin Mary commented to me, "Imagine having one of your first things to do on arrival to a new country is bury your child."

We know that they were permitted to stay in America and would end up in Chicago. They lived for a time on Roscoe Street, a couple of blocks from Wrigley Field, in an apartment building they shared with six other families. Just as we noted in an earlier chapter about people of German descent tending to end up in the same neighborhood enclaves, the same was true for those from Persia.

As my cousin Mary said in our conversation about the matter, "If you were from the same town in the Old Country, you were like family." John was a bricklayer doing projects all across the country. They had four children, the youngest of whom, Esther, married my Uncle John. My cousin Chris would follow a career path similar to that of his grandpa; instead of bricklaying, he became a stonemason. My relationship with Chris is the reason I have included the story of his grandparents. Chris passionately talks about them and wants the younger generation of his family to know their history.

On October 5, 1937, John signed a Declaration of Intention to become a United States citizen. My cousin Beth told me in conversation that her Grandpa John was always expressing appreciation for being an American. He would often ask, "What have you done for your country today?"

CHAPTER 10

BIBLICAL CITIZENSHIP

I n the previous chapters I have given a lot of consideration to citizenship as it pertains to immigrants, ancestors, and our country. Now I wish to address a truth set forth in the Bible that applies to Christians. My desire is that this will be meaningful to all readers, but I recognize that not all identify as Christian. For those who don't, the idea of being a citizen of heaven is probably foreign to you. That doesn't have to be the case for you if you believe in Christ as your Savior and Lord, as I have earlier pointed out (in chapter 4 within my personal testimony and in chapter 7 on liberty). Keep in mind, too, that there are a number of truths from Scripture that explain what is true for those that know the Lord Jesus Christ as Savior. The believer has redemption, reconciliation, and forgiveness, just to name a few of these benefits.

We have a standing with our Lord that is granted to us strictly on the basis of grace (as opposed to any merit of our own). These blessings and benefits can be divided neatly into the "positional" and the "possessional." Positional gifts include the believer being united with Christ in His death, burial, resurrection, and ascension and being seated with Him in His glory (I invite you to pursue an understanding of these realities in the Bible in Romans 6:3–11 and Ephesians 2:4–10; the words "positional" and "possessional" are not in the Bible, but the underlying information from which these concepts derive is there.) Citizenship, on the other hand, is given to us as a possession, along with our gaining an inheritance and being made heirs with Christ in eternity. Once an individual trusts in the finished work of Christ for salvation, they are incorporated into the body of Christ, His Church.

There are many facets of salvation and of New Testament grace-living—too many to address here. I owe my limited understanding to my own reading and study but also to a good friend and pastor/teacher, Tim Hoelscher. Tim is a pastor in Royal City, Washington, who faithfully and consistently teaches the Bible and has written some helpful books as well; you can access aspects of his ministry at www.graceteaching.com and YouTube at GraceTeaching1703.

When considering the Bible's historical sections and comparing them to what has taken place all throughout history, you will note its repeated references to war, famine, plagues, and natural disasters. God dealt with nations in the past and will continue to do so in the future. From the Tower of Babel in Genesis 11 to the call of Abram in Genesis 12 to Jesus telling His disciples to go to all nations to preach the gospel (Matthew 28:19), we see that He is sovereign over all nations. The prophesies regarding Israel will be fulfilled. Israel has promises of land that they have yet to be given. These promises are not for the Church. Israel's promises are earthly, the church's are spiritual and heavenly.

We as believers are "blessed . . . with every spiritual blessing in the heavenly places in Christ" (Ephesians 1:3). Incidentally, an easy way to search out and find the positional and possessional blessings in the New Testament is to follow the prepositions "in," "into," and "together with" (sometimes called the "in-

Christ" truths). An example is the "in Christ" in the verse quoted immediately above. The point is that citizenship is just one element of many that explains the believer's identity and defines the way we should live. "Our citizenship," says the apostle Paul, "is in heaven, from which we also eagerly wait for a Savior, the Lord Jesus Christ" (Philippians 3:20).

Apart from believing the gospel of Christ, an individual is an outsider, or a foreigner (Ephesians 2:12) to this citizenship. With salvation, however, Christians share a common citizenship and can now participate fully in the body of Christ. Nothing can nullify that citizenship for the believer, and there is nothing about our heavenly citizenship that can be imposed on an earthly citizenship.

Although we have touched briefly in this book on immigrants being deported, we have not delved into instances in which individuals have been stripped of their citizenship. That is called denaturalization or the revocation of naturalization. That can happen for various reasons, but an example would be if someone were sentenced for war crimes. I mention this here only to contrast this revocation of citizenship to the eternal kingdom citizenship enjoyed by the Christian, which can never be renounced.

There are some parallels between earthly citizenship and a Christian's heavenly citizenship. In both we are granted rights and privileges and given responsibilities. Kingdom citizenship in Christ becomes the basis for the way we live and treat others; in a more limited sense, of course, this is also true of responsible citizenship within a country. In Philippians 1:27 the word "conduct" (*politeumai* in the Greek) refers to behavior as a citizen. In 2 Timothy 4:18 the apostle Paul wrote, "The Lord will rescue me from every evil deed, and will bring me safely to His heavenly kingdom; to Him be glory forever and ever. Amen."

In a kingdom one naturally expects rulership and a sense of citizenship under that rule.

While participating here on earth as a "citizen of heaven," we are called by Peter to be "a chosen people, a royal priesthood, a holy nation, a people for God's own possession, that you may proclaim the excellencies of Him who has called you out of darkness into His marvelous light; for you once were not a people, but now you are the people of God; you had not received mercy, but now you have received mercy" (1 Peter 2:9–10).

Considering what I now possess as a believer in Christ, you can understand why I am thankful for something so much greater, as I shared in the beginning of this book. What I have goes infinitely deeper than the roots of blood ties or religious tradition. Trusting in the eternal truths of God's Word provides not only what is better but what is best—all by His grace.

It is interesting to note that early Christians, even though they were "citizens of heaven," had a use for their earthly citizenship, just as we do. Paul provides us an example in Acts 16:37 when he exercised his freedom as a Roman citizen to say to the jailer who was sent to release him, "After beating us in public without due process—men who are Romans—they threw us into prison; and now they are releasing us secretly? No indeed! On the contrary, let them come in person and lead us out."

Then again in Acts 22:27–29, Paul spoke to a commander who had "acquired this citizenship for a large sum of money," to which Paul replied, "But I was actually born a citizen." The commander became worried that he had broken the law, and in the end Paul made use of his own Roman citizenship when he made an "appeal to Caesar" (Acts 25:11). Paul knew that, as a Roman citizen, he should have been exempt from the kind of treatment he had received when he was tortured and imprisoned without trial.

Along with living as "citizens of heaven," we are also given instruction in Scripture as to what our attitude should be toward government authority:

> Every person is to be subject to the governing authorities. For there is no authority except from God, and those which exist are established by God. Therefore whoever resists authority has opposed the ordinance of God; and they who have opposed will receive condemnation upon themselves. For rulers are not a cause of fear for good behavior, but for evil. Do you want to have no fear of authority? Do what is good and you will have praise from the same; for it is a servant of God to you for good. But if you do what is evil, be afraid; for it does not bear the sword for nothing; for it is a servant of God, an avenger who brings wrath on the one who practices evil. Therefore it is necessary to be in subjection, not only because of wrath, but also for the sake of conscience. For because of this you also pay taxes, for rulers are servants of God, devoting themselves to this very thing. Pay to all what is due them: tax to whom tax is due; custom to whom custom; respect to whom respect; honor to whom honor. (Romans 13:1–7)

If there are times when others try to intimidate or slander the believer, we are told how to handle it:

> And who is there to harm you if you prove zealous for what is good? But even if you should suffer for the sake of righteousness, you are blessed. And do not fear their

intimidation, and do not be in dread, but sanctify Christ as Lord in your hearts, always being ready to make a defense to everyone who asks you to give an account for the hope that is in you, but with gentleness and reverence; and keep a good conscience so that in the thing in which you are slandered, those who disparage your good behavior in Christ will be put to shame. For it is better, if God should will it so, that you suffer for doing what is right rather than for doing what is wrong. (1 Peter 3:13–17)

The response we give to governing authorities and others should also be tempered by the example of the stance Peter and John took in Acts 4:18–20 when they were commanded not to "speak or teach at all in the name of Jesus. But Peter and John answered and said to them, 'Whether it is right in the sight of God to listen to you rather than to God, make your own judgment; for we cannot stop speaking about what we have seen and heard.'" From Scripture we are shown what our attitude and response toward earthly authority should be, but we are also enjoined to actively pray for those who have been granted authority over us (1 Timothy 2:1–3).[221] Why? So "that we might lead a tranquil and quiet life."

The Bible uses several different words to describe our time on the earth: *alien, resident, foreigner, pilgrim, exile, stranger,* and *sojourner.* They are all used to remind us that this earth is not really our home (see, e.g., Hebrews 11:13; 1 Peter 1:1; 2:11). That doesn't mean we should shut ourselves off and not care about the direction of the culture and nation.

I have heard it said, "You know we are not labeled Democrats or Republicans in heaven." I realize that this statement is intended to help us resist being argumentative, antagonistic, divisive, or hateful toward those with opposing views. But that doesn't mean we shouldn't care about either the issues or the people. We know from Jesus's words that there is no marriage in heaven, either: "For in the resurrection they neither marry nor are given in marriage" (Matthew 22:30). Of course we would never encourage people to not care about their marriages.

C. S. Lewis in his book *Mere Christianity* includes a passage that is sometimes referred to as his "argument from desire"; online discussions about it are available. Lewis wrote, "If we find ourselves with a desire that nothing in this world can satisfy, the most probable explanation is that we are made for another world."[222] The biblical idea of being a "citizen of heaven" assures us of the reality of that world.

When thinking of that world, and the desire for it, I am reminded of chapter 2 of this book and the discussion of the push/pull factors of immigration. In a similar way, Christians have a variety of reasons to long for that new world. In our time here, despite our experiences of joy, peace, beauty, goodness, life, liberty, and happiness—we still face the push, so to speak, of suffering, pain, sin, trials, disease, perils, distress, afflictions, difficulties, and hardships. Yet we at the same time experience the longing and the pull of hope and promise.

In Philippians the apostle Paul has this to say: "For our citizenship is in heaven, from which we also eagerly wait for a Savior, the Lord Jesus Christ; who will transform the body of our lowly condition into conformity with His glorious body, by the exertion of the power that He has even to subject all things to Himself" (Philippians 3:20–21). Consider also Paul's rousing words from Romans 8:18: "I consider that the sufferings of this present time are not worthy to be compared with the glory that is to be revealed to us."

I close with a quote I came across in Jan Karon's *Patches of Godlight*. The book is a collection of her "favorite quotes" from her fictional character, Father Tim:

> We are not citizens of this world trying to make our way to heaven; we are citizens of heaven trying to make our way through this world. That radical Christian insight can be life-changing. We are not to live so as to earn God's love, inherit heaven, and purchase (or earn) our salvation. All those are given to us as gifts; gifts bought by Jesus on the cross and handed over to us (given by His grace). We are to live as God's redeemed, as heirs of heaven, and as citizens of another land: the kingdom of God . . . We live as those who are on a journey home; a home we know will have the lights on and the door open and our Father waiting for us when we arrive. That means in all adversity our worship of God is joyful, our life is hopeful, our future is secure. There is nothing we can lose on earth that can rob us of the treasures God has given and will give us.[223]

ACKNOWLEDGMENTS

First, I want to point out that at no time was artificial intelligence used in the writing of this book, at least not on purpose. I wonder what the end result would have been had AI written it. No, only natural average intelligence was used (NAI).

Second, a special thanks to my wife, Crystal, for her advice and patience. Third, my thanks goes out for the help given by editor Donna Huisien at Credo House Publishers. I am also grateful to those who wish to remain anonymous.

I appreciated the tidbits of information gleaned from ancestry.com that helped fill in some gaps.

I am reminded of the assistance of one Mildred Rugger, who gave of her time to tutor me in writing while I was in college so I could pass the Writing Competency Test—is that still a requirement?

I do not consider myself particularly competent in writing, but I felt I had something important to share, so, here I am with a book. Who would have ever thought? Or, as Al Weitz would have said, "Who would have thunked it?" Only in America!

ONLINE RESOURCES

- Visit *uscis.gov/tools* for a list of online services.
- Check your case status: *uscis.gov/casestatus.*
- Change your address: *uscis.gov/addresschange.*
- Submit an online request about your case: *uscis.gov/e-request.*
- Check case processing times: *uscis.gov/processingtimes.*
- Sign up for automatic updates on your case: my account. *uscis.dhs.gov.*
- Ask Emma, a virtual assistant, your immigration questions: *uscis.gov/emma.*
- Explore your immigration options: *my.uscis.gov/exploremyoptions.*
- Find free forms: *uscis.gov/forms.*
- USCIS contact center: 1-800-375-5283.
- For those who are deaf, hard of hearing, or have a speech disability: TTY 1-800-767-1833.

BIBLIOGRAPHY

About CBP. (n.d.). US Customs And Border Protection. https://www. cbp.gov/about#:~:text=With%20more%20than%2060%2C000% 20employees,lawful%20international%20travel%20and%20trade.

American Gaming Association. (n.d.). https://www.americangaming.org.

Armenian Genocide (1915–1923). (n.d.). https://www.armenian-genocide.org/genocide.html.

Arthur, A. (2024, March 15). Biden promised to open the border as a candidate in 2020—now he laughs at you about it. *New York Post.* https://nypost.com/2024/03/15/opinion/the-promises-biden-made-to-keep-the-border-open/.

Asylum, USCIS. (2025, January 24). USCIS. https://www.uscis.gov/ humanitarian/refugees-and-asylum/asylum.

Avildsen, J. G. (Director). (1976). *Rocky.* Paramount Theaters.

Bar. Affiliated with the Local History Network of the State Historical Society of Iowa, and the Iowa Museum Association. (n.d.). In *The Encyclopedia of Dubuque.*

Barnhart, C. L. (1960). *Thorndike-Barnhart Comprehensive Desk Dictionary.*

Batalova, J. (2024, March 13). *Frequently Requested Statistics on Immigrants and Immigration in the United States.* Migration Policy. Retrieved March 13, 2024, from https://www.migrationpolicy. org/article/frequently-requested-statistics-immigrants-and-immigration-united-states-2024.

Baxter, A. M., & Nowrasteh, A. (2021, August 23). *A Brief History of US Immigration Policy from the Colonial Period to the Present Day.* Cato Institute. https://doi.org/10.36009/PA.919.

Beck, G., & Haskins, J. T. (2022). *The Great Reset: Joe Biden and the Rise of Twenty-First-Century Fascism*. Simon and Schuster.

Becoming a British citizen. (n.d.). Citizens Advice. https://www.citizensadvice.org.uk/immigration/getting-british-citizenship/becoming-a-british-citizen/.

Bergman, A. (2025, January 7). *207 Gambling Addiction Statistics & Facts 2024*. Quit Gamble. https://quitgamble.com/gambling-addiction-statistics-and-facts/.

Berkin, C. (2015). *The Bill of Rights: The Fight to Secure America's Liberties*. Simon and Schuster.

"Biden-Harris administration has intentionally left us vulnerable": Pfluger, Higgins deliver opening statements in hearing on terror threats from the border—Committee on Homeland Security. (2024, September 19). https://homeland.house.gov/2024/09/19/biden-harris-administration-has-intentionally-left-us-vulnerable-pfluger-higgins-deliver-opening-statements-in-hearing-on-terror-threats-from-the-border/.

Boubil, A. (Director). (n.d.). *Les Miserables* [Musical Theater].

Branch, G. (2025, February 14). Teaching evolution has a bright future in the US *Scientific American*. https://www.scientificamerican.com/article/teaching-evolution-has-a-bright-future-in-the-u-s/#:~:text=In%20short%2C%20a%20century%20after,in%20the%20light%20of%20evolution.

Brenan, B. M. (2025, February 26). More than six in 10 Americans drink alcohol.

Gallup.com. https://news.gallup.com/poll/509501/six-americans-drink-alcohol.aspx.

Chin, G. J. (2024). The "Free White Person" Clause of the Naturalization Act of 1790 as Super-Statute. *The William and Mary Law Review*, 65(5).

Cohen, E. F. (2020). *Illegal: How America's Lawless Immigration Regime Threatens Us All*. Basic Books.

COMISKEY PARK—Encyclopedia Dubuque. (n.d.). https://www.encyclopediadubuque.org/index.php/COMISKEY_PARK.

Committee on the Judiciary, & Subcommittee on Immigration Integrity, Security, and Enforcement. (2024). *INSIDE THE BIDEN-HARRIS ADMINISTRATION'S OPEN-BORDERS ALLIANCE WITH UNITED NATIONS BUREAUCRATS.* https://judiciary.house.gov/sites/evo-subsites/republicans-judiciary.house.gov/files/evo-media-document/2024-11-01%20Inside%20the%20Biden-Harris%20Administration%27s%20Open-Borders%20Alliance%20with%20United%20Nations%20Bureaucrats.pdf.

Cook, B. (2024, September 12). *Fact Sheet: Planned Parenthood's 2022–23 Annual Report*—Lozier Institute. Lozier Institute. https://lozierinstitute.org/fact-sheet-planned-parenthoods-2022-23-annual-report/#:~:text=The%20number%20of%20patients%20(2.05,%25%20(1%2C721)%2C%20respectively.

Council on Foreign Relations. (n.d.). Council on Foreign Relations. https://www.cfr.org/.

Creation role and purpose of Republican Government. (n.d.). Bill of Rights Institute. https://billofrightsinstitute.org/essays/republican-government/.

DALZELL, Wilbur—*Encyclopedia Dubuque.* (n.d.). https://www.encyclopediadubuque.org/index.php/DALZELL,_Wilbur.

De Relaciones Exteriores, S. (n.d.). *Double nationality.* gob.mx. https://www.gob.mx/sre/documentos/double-nationality#:~:text=Is%20dual%20nationality%20allowed%20in,rights%20for%20the%20dual%20national.

De Vise, D. (2023, June 5). *Americans are drinking as much alcohol now as in Civil War Days [Online forum post].* The Hill. https://thehill.com/policy/healthcare/4043030-hard-liquor-consumption-is-up-60-percent-since-the-1990s/.

Declaration of Independence: a transcription. (2024, December 30). National Archives. https://www.archives.gov/founding-docs/declaration-transcript.

Defiance Publishing. (2023, August 11). *What Is a Conservative Christian?* Defiance Press and Publishing. https://defiancepress. com/news/what-is-a-conservative-christian/.

Department of Justice. (2001). The USA PATRIOT Act: Preserving Life and Liberty. In *The USA PATRIOT Act: Preserving Life and Liberty.* https://www.justice.gov/archive/ll/what_is_the_patriot_act.pdf.

Dictionary.com, Meanings & Definitions of English Words. (n.d.). In Dictionary.com.https://www.dictionary.com/browse/fake%20news.

Dictionary.com, Meanings & Definitions of English Words. (2025). In Dictionary.com https://www.dictionary.com/browse/tribalism.

Diversity, Equity & Inclusion. (2022, August 11). McKinsey & Company. https://www.mckinsey.com/capabilities/people-and-organizational-performance/how-we-help-clients/diversity-equity-and-inclusion.

Dorchak, P. (2008, December 19). Soon to be 90, Gloden is an old Bird who still roots for Eagles. *https://www.inquirer.com.* https://www. inquirer.com/philly/sports/playbook/20081219_Soon_to_be_90__Gloden_is_an_old_Bird_who_still_roots_for_Eagles.html.

Dred Scott v. Sandford (1857). (2024, July 8). National Archives. https:// www.archives.gov/milestone-documents/dred-scott-v-sandford.

Dubuque, IA—*Official Website, Official website.* (n.d.). https://www. cityofdubuque.org/.

Duignan, & Brian. (2025, January 30). *Identity politics | Definition, Examples, & Facts.* Encyclopedia Britannica. https://www.britannica. com/topic/identity-politicsl

Election integrity | The Heritage Foundation. (n.d.). The Heritage Foundation. https://www.heritage.org/election-integrityl

Encyclopedia Dubuque. (n.d.). https://www.encyclopediadubuque.org/l

Facts about excessive drinking. (2024, October 7). Drink Less, Be Your Best. https://www.cdc.gov/drink-less-be-your-best/facts-about-excessive-drinking/index.html#:~:text=Understanding%20excessive%20drinking&text=It%20includes%3A,by%20people%20younger%20than%2021.

Father Flanagan, Boys Town. (n.d.). Boys Town. https://www.boystown.org/history/father-flanagan.

Friedman, M. (2020). *Capitalism and freedom.*

Gabbard, T. (2024). *For love of country: Leave the Democrat Party Behind.* Simon and Schuster.

Gaming and gambling. (n.d.). https://responsiblegambling.org/for-the-public/safer-play/gaming-and-gambling/.

Geiger, A. (2025, January 27). What the data says about immigrants in the US *Pew Research Center.* https://www.pewresearch.org/short-reads/2024/09/27/key-findings-about-us-immigrants/

German Americans' contributions to our nation | AmericansAll. (n.d.). https://americansall.org/legacy-partner/german-americans-contributions-our-nation.

German Immigration and Relocation in US History. Building a New Nation. (n.d.). [Slide show; Website]. Library of Congress. https://www.loc.gov/classroom-materials/immigration/german/building-a-new-nation/#:~:text=By%20the%20middle%20of%20the,number%20only%20to%20the%20English.

Gilbert, & Adrian. (2025, January 10). *Battle of Monte Cassino (1944) | Description & facts.* Encyclopedia Britannica. https://www.britannica.com/topic/Battle-of-Monte-Cassino.

Grant, G. (2000). *Grand Illusions: The Legacy of Planned Parenthood.* Cumberland House Publishing.

Gul Djemal Lands Citizens: Steerage Passengers Return to Ship Today from Fumigation Camp. (n.d.). *New York Times.* https://www.nytimes.com/1920/11/03/archives/gul-djemal-lands-citizens-steerage-passengers-return-to-ship-today.html.

Haass, R. (2023). *The Bill of Obligations: The Ten Habits of Good Citizens*. Penguin.

Hall, M. D. (2019). *Did America have a Christian founding? Separating Modern Myth from Historical Truth*. HarperChristian + ORM.

Hankinson, S. (n.d.). *Tren de Aragua Is the Latest Transnational Criminal Organization to Establish Itself in the US* | The Heritage Foundation. The Heritage Foundation. https://www.heritage.org/ border-security/report/tren-de-aragua-the-latest-transnational-criminal-organization-establish.

Hanson, V. D. (2021). *The Dying Citizen: How Progressive Elites, Tribalism, and Globalization Are Destroying the Idea of America*. Basic Books.

Harriet Beecher Stowe Meets Lincoln. (1862, November 25). Civil War on the Western Border. https://civilwaronthewesternborder.org/ timeline/harriet-beecher-stowe-meets-lincoln.

Higley & John. (2016, November 30). *Elites | Power, Privilege & Social Stratification*. Encyclopedia Britannica. https://www.britannica. com/topic/elite-sociology.

History and Immigration. History of German-American Relations-1683-1900. (n.d.). *History and Immigration*.

History.com Editorial Staff. (2018, May 7). Printing Press—Invented, Gutenberg, Significance.*History.com*. Retrieved March 3, 2025, from https://www.history.com/topics/inventions/printing-press.

Home, AmericansAll. (n.d.). https://www.americansall.org/.

Home, Library of Congress. (n.d.). The Library of Congress. https:// www.loc.gov/.

Horowitz, D. (2019). *Dark Agenda: The War to Destroy Christian America*.

Household debt and credit report. (n.d.). FEDERAL RESERVE BANK of NEW YORK. https://www.newyorkfed.org/microeconomics/ hhdc.html.

How prevalent is pornography? (n.d.). Institute for Family Studies. https://ifstudies.org/blog/how-prevalent-is-pornography.

How to Identify Critical Race Theory, The Heritage Foundation. (n.d.). The Heritage Foundation. https://www.heritage.org/civil-society/heritage-explains/how-identify-critical-race-theory.

Immigrants Arriving in New York City 1887 Engraving (Digital Vision Vectors) via Getty images. (n.d.).

Jewison, N. (Director). (1978). *F.I.S.T.* Filmex.

Journey to America. (n.d.). Spartacus Educational. https://spartacus-educational.com/USAEjourney.htm.

Justice Ruth Bader Ginsburg Offers Critique of Roe v. Wade During Law School Visit | University of Chicago Law School. (2022, May 11). University of Chicago Law School. https://www.law.uchicago.edu/news/justice-ruth-bader-ginsburg-offers-critique-roe-v-wade-during-law-school-visit.

Karon, J. (2002). *Patches of Godlight: Father Tim's Favorite Quotes*. Viking.

Kelly, J. (2023). *The Anti-Communist manifesto*. Simon and Schuster.

Kwasky, A. (1971). *The Old Lady in Dubuque*. Vintage Press.

Lalami, L. (2021). *Conditional Citizens: On Belonging in America*. Vintage.

Larson, E. (2024). *The Demon of Unrest: A Saga of Hubris, Heartbreak, and Heroism at the Dawn of the Civil War*. Crown.

Laurie, C. D. (1994). Goebbels's Iowan: Frederick W. Kaltenbach and Nazi Short-Wave Radio Broadcasts to America, 1939–1945. *The Annals of Iowa*, 53(3), 219–245. https://doi.org/10.17077/0003-4827.9815.

Leopold, D. (1975). *Dubuque Folklore: A Contribution from American Trust and Savings Bankto Dubuqueland in Celebration of Our Nations Bicentennial*. The Bank.

Lewis, C. S. (2001). *Mere Christianity* . In Collins eBooks.

Main page—*Ballotpedia*. (n.d.). https://ballotpedia.org/Main_Page.

McAllister, R. (2025, January 2). *11 most common reasons for divorce & Why marriages end*. North American Community Hub. https://nchstats.com/common-reasons-for-divorce/.

Medication abortion: Your questions answered. (2023, September 11). Yale Medicine. https://www.yalemedicine.org/news/medication-abortion-your-questions-answered.

Men's Group. (n.d.). *15 Mind-Blowing Statistics about Pornography and the Church.* https://mensgroup.ca/blog/f/15-mind-blowing-statistics-about-pornography-and-the-church.

Merriam-Webster. (n.d.). *Dictionary by Merriam-Webster.* https://www.merriamwebster.com/.

Merriam-Webster. (2022). *The Merriam-Webster Dictionary.* Merriam-Webster.

Milestones in the History of US Foreign Relations—Office of the Historian. (n.d.). https://history.state.gov/milestones/1945-1952/immigration-act#:~:text=the%20full%20notice.-,The%20Immigration%20and%20Nationality%20Act%20of%201952%20(The%20McCarran%2DWalter,controversial%20system%20of%20immigrant%20selection.

Narea, N. (2024, June 3). America's misunderstood border crisis, in 8 charts. *Vox.* https://www.vox.com/politics/24153132/us-border-crisis-mexico-migrant-immigration-asylum.

National Immigration Forum. (2021, June 23). *Fact Sheet: Overview of the Special Immigrant Visa Programs—National Immigration Forum.* https://immigrationforum.org/article/fact-sheet-overview-of-the-special-immigrant-visa-programs/#:~:text=SIVs%20are%20available%20to%20individuals,one%20of%20two%20SIV%20programs.

National Right to Life. (2024, February 19). *National Right to Life Releases Eleventh Annual Report: The State of Abortion in the United States—National Right to Life.* National Right to Life—Protecting Life in America Since 1968. https://nrlc.org/nrlnewstoday/2024/02/national-right-to-life-releases-eleventh-annual-report-the-state-of-abortion-in-the-united-states/.

Orwell, G. (1949). *Nineteen Eighty-Four: A Novel.*

Ostberg & René. (2025, January 9). *Transhumanism, Definition, History, Ethics, Philosophy, & Facts*. Encyclopedia Britannica. https://www.britannica.com/topic/transhumanism.

Othfors, D. (n.d.). *Germanic*—TGOL. https://thegreatoceanliners.com/articles/germanic/.

Oversight Committee Republicans Verified Account. (2024, February 22). Hearing wrap up: Biden administration's catch and release operation has inflamed the raging crisis at the southern border—United States House Committee on Oversight and Accountability. United States House Committee on Oversight and Accountability. https://oversight.house.gov/release/hearing-wrap-up-biden-administrations-catch-and-release-operation-has-inflamed-the-raging-crisis-at-the-southern-border%EF%BF%BC/.

Parker, N. H. (n.d.). *Iowa as It Is in 1855; A Gazetteer for Citizens and a Hand-book for Immigrants: Embracing a Full Description of the State of Iowa: Her agricultural, mineralogical, and geological character: Her water courses, Timberlands, soil and climate; Railroad lines built and projected, number of churches and schools in each County; Population and Business Statistics of the Most Important Cities and Towns.*

Pestritto, R. (n.d.). *The Birth of the Administrative State: Where it came from and what it means for limited government, The Heritage Foundation.* The Heritage Foundation. https://www.heritage.org/political-process/report/the-birth-the-administrative-state-where-it-came-and-what-it-means-limited.

Peterson Foundation. (2025, February 24). *National Debt Clock: What is the national debt right now?* https://www.pgpf.org/national-debt-clock/.

Planned Parenthood's Reckoning with Margaret Sanger. (2021, April 28). Planned Parenthood. https://www.plannedparenthood.org/planned-parenthood-pacific-southwest/blog/planned-parenthoods-reckoning-with-margaret-sanger.

Public papers—George Bush Library and Museum. (n.d.). https://bush41library.tamu.edu/archives/public-papers/2217.

Quiet Amnesty: How the Biden-Harris administration uses the nation's immigration courts to advance an Open-Borders agenda, House Judiciary Committee Republicans. (2024, October 24). House Judiciary Committee Republicans. https://judiciary.house.gov/media/press-releases/quiet-amnesty-how-biden-harris-administration-uses-nations-immigration-courts.

Ramaswamy, V. (2023). *Woke, Inc: Inside Corporate America's Social Justice Scam.*

Ranji, U., Diep, K., & Salganicoff, A. (2025, February 27). *Key facts on abortion in the United States | KFF.* KFF. https://www.kff.org/womens-health-policy/issue-brief/key-facts-on-abortion-in-the-united-states/.

Reagan, R. (1967, January 5). *Inaugural Address.* Inauguration of the President of the United States of America. https://www.reaganlibrary.gov/archives/speech/january-5-1967-inaugural-address-public-ceremony.

Reid & A, S. (2025, February 12). *Conspiracy Theory, Definition, Examples, & Facts.* Encyclopedia Britannica. https://www.britannica.com/topic/conspiracy-theory.

RIVERBOAT GAMBLING—Encyclopedia Dubuque. (n.d.). https:www.encyclopediadubuque.org/index.php/RIVERBOAT_GAMBLING.

Roth, C. (2023). *You Will Own Nothing: Your War with a New Financial Order and How to FightBack.* Broadside Books.

Ruane, M. E. (2019, April 30). Brief History of the Enduring Phony Science that Perpetuates White Supremacy. *The Washington Post.* Retrieved January 30, 2024, from https://www.washingtonpost.com/local/a-brief-history-of-the-enduring-phony-science-that-perpetuates-white-supremacy/2019/04/29/20e6aef0-5aeb-11e9-a00e-050dc7b82693_story.html.

Ruiz Soto, A. G. & Migration Policy Institute. (2024). *Immigrants and Crime in the United States.* https://www.migrationpolicy.org/sites/

default/files/publications/mpi-explainer-immigration-crime-2024_
final.pdf.

Schweizer, P. (2024). *Blood Money: Why the Powerful Turn a Blind Eye
While China Kills Americans*. Harper.

Services, U. C. a. I., Security, D. O. H., & Office, U. G. P. (2025). *Welcome
to the United States: a guide for new immigrants*. Aegitas.

Silverstein, J. (2021, November 9). The 1619 project and the battle over
US history. *The New York Times*. Retrieved November 12, 2021, from
https://www.nytimes.com/2021/11/09/magazine/1619-project-us-
history.html.

Spiro, P. J. (2019). *Citizenship: What Everyone Needs to Know*.

Spurbeck, D. K. (1999). *The Christian "In Christ": An Introduction to
"In Christ" Truth: The Believer's Position and Possessions in Christ*.
Know to Grow "In Christ" Publications.

Stanley, J. (2020). *How Fascism Works: The Politics of Us and Them*.
Random House Trade Paperbacks.

*Startling Fact Sheet: Encounters of Chinese nationals surpass all fiscal 2023
at the Southwest border*. (2024, April 18). https://homeland.house.
gov/2024/04/18/startling-stats-factsheet-encounters-of-chinese-
nationals-surpass-all-fiscal-year-2023-at-the-southwest-border/.

Stowe, H. B. (1852). *Uncle Tom's Cabin*.

Streaks, J. (2025, January 6). *Average American Debt: Household Debt
Statistics*. Business Insider. https://www.businessinsider.com/
personal-finance/credit-score/average-american-debt.

Street, W. (2021, September 8). Heavy Drinking in America: Cities
with High Alcohol Consumption. USA TODAY. https://www.
usatoday.com/picture-gallery/life/2021/09/08/the-50-drunkest-
cities-in-america/118462502/.

Streeter Aldrich, B. (1917). *Song of Years*. Appleton-Century Co.

Streeter Aldrich, B. (1959). A Bess Streeter Aldrich Treasury. In *I
Remember, A Short Story* (I). Appleton Century—Crofts Inc.

Tanz, L. J., Stewart, A., Gladden, R. M., Ko, J. Y., Owens, L., & O'Donnell,
J. (2024). Detection of illegally manufactured fentanyls and

carfentanil in drug overdose deaths—United States, 2021–2024. *MMWR Morbidity and Mortality Weekly Report*, 73(48), 1099–1105. https://doi.org/10.15585/mmwr.mm7348a2.

Team, E. (2024, July 5). Church of the Holy Trinity v. United States (1892). *The Free Speech Center.* https://firstamendment.mtsu.edu/article/church-of-the-holy-trinity-v-united-states/.

Technopolis. (n.d.). In *Collins English Dictionary.* https://www.collinsdictionary.com/dictionary/english/technopolis.

The Associated Press. (2022, June 24). *Excerpts from the Supreme Court's landmark abortion decision, AP News. AP News.* https://apnews.com/article/abortion-us-supreme-court-health-samuel-alito-66c301d223759e842ad95e89f597d587#:~:text=JUSTICE%20SAMUEL%20ALITO'S%20MAJORITY%20OPINION,decision%20has%20had%20damaging%20consequences.

The Corporate Governance Institute. (2023, November 28). A simple guide to ESG—*The Corporate Governance Institute.* https://www.thecorporategovernanceinstitute.com/insights/guides/simple-guide.esgsrsltid=AfmBOopN9bzfrNFQv5vmNiQcV66N5o 3FMtykTeFs q8egyooREURWEiY6

The Editors of Encyclopaedia Britannica. (2023, May 1). *Italian Campaign | Summary, Map, Significance, Date, & World War II.* Encyclopedia Britannica. https://britannica.com/topic/Italian-Campaign#/media/1/297181/279620.

The Electoral College. (2023, July 27). National Archives. https://www.archives.gov/electoral-college#:~:text=It's%20a%20Process%2C%20not%20a%20Place&text=Acting%20as%20an%20intermediary%2C%20it,of%20electoral%20votes%20in%20Congress.

The Fed Explained. (n.d.). https://www.federalreserve.gov/aboutthefed/the-fed-explained.htm.

The history & Impact of Planned Parenthood. (n.d.). Planned Parenthood. https://www.plannedparenthood.org/about-us/who-we-are/our-history.

The New Colossus—Statue of Liberty National Monument (US National Park Service). (n.d.). https://www.nps.gov/stli/learn/historyculture/colossus.htm#:~:text=%22Give%20me%20your%20tired%2C%20your,refuse%20of%20your%20teeming%20shore.

The US divorce rate has hit a 50-Year low. (n.d.). Institute for Family Studies. https://ifstudies.org/blog/the-us-divorce-rate-has-hit-a-50-year-low.

The Works of Benjamin Franklin, including the Private as well as the Official and Scientific Correspondence, Together with the Unmutilated and Correct Version of the Autobiography, compiled and edited by John Bigelow (New York: G.P. Putnam's Sons, 1904). The Federal Edition in 12 volumes. Vol. VII (Letters and Misc. Writings 1775–1779).

Tidwell, M., C. O., Welte, J. W., Barnes, G. M., & Dayanim, B. (1991). Gambling Modes and State Gambling Laws: Changes to 1999 to 2011 and Beyond. *National Library of Medicine*. https://doi.org/10.1089/glre.2014.1914.PMID:27688682:PMCID:PMC5012365.

Tiggers, J. T., & Shaffer, J. L. (2000). *Dubuque, Iowa: Then and Now* (1st ed.). Arcadia Publishing.

Tobin, N., Ph.D. (1985, May 22). *Comments Given at the Funeral of Margaret Winders. Funeral of Margaret Winders*, Dubuque, United States of America. Sacred Heart Church

Topic: Sports betting in the US (2025, February 10). Statista. https://www.statista.com/topics/8581/sports-betting-us/.

Transforming Our world: the 2030 Agenda for Sustainable Development, Department of Economic and Social Affairs. (n.d.). https://sdgs.un.org/2030agenda.

Treuer, D. (2022, November 7). *Do We Have the History of Native Americans Backward?* The New Yorker. https://www.newyorker.com/magazine/2022/11/14/do-we-have-the-history-of-native-americans-backward-indigenous-continent.

Understanding Transgender people, gender identity, and gender expression. (2023). *American Psychological Association*.

US Department of Defense. (n.d.). *The Purple Heart: America's Oldest Medal.* https://www.defense.gov/News/Feature-Stories/story/Article/1650949/the-purple-heart-americas-oldest-medal/.

US government agencies involved in the immigration process. (2017, August 31). The Visa Firm. https://thevisafirm.com/dc-immigration-lawyer/us-government-agencies-involved/

USCIS. (2022). 10 steps to naturalization. In *M-1051.* https://www.uscis.gov/sites/default/files/document/brochures/M-1051.pdf.

Waldman, S. (2009). *Founding Faith: How Our Founding Fathers Forged a Radical New Approach to Religious Liberty.* Random House Trade Paperbacks.

Walsh, P., Dr. (2016, May 19). *Who Remembers the Persians?* Pat Walsh. https://drpatwalsh.com/2016/05/07/who-remembers-the-persians/.

Warfare 1914–1918 (Ottoman Empire/Middle East)/1.0/handbook—1914-1918-Online (WW1) Encyclopedia. (2024, July 9). 1914-1918-Online (WW1) Encyclopedia. https://encyclopedia.1914-1918-online.net/article/warfare-1914-1918-ottoman-empiremiddle-east/.

Wende, P. (1985). *History of Germany.* Macmillan Essential Histories.

White, E. B. (1970). *The Trumpet of the Swan.*

Wiegand, I., Cade, S., Pond, J., & Woodman De Lazo, V. (2016). *FUNDAMENTALS OF IMMIGRATION LAW.* https://www.justice.gov/sites/default/files/pages/attachments/2016/03/03/fundamentals_of_immigration_law_-_feb_2016.pdf#:~:text=FUNDAMENTALS%20OF%20IMMIGRATION%20LAW.%20by%20.%20Charles%20A.

Wikipedia contributors. (2024, December 21). *Media bias in the United States.* Wikipedia. https://en.wikipedia.org/w/index.php?=Media_bias_in_the_United_States&oldid=1264369635.

World Economic Forum. (n.d.). https://www.weforum.org/about/history/.

World Health Organization (WHO). (n.d.). Who We Are. https://www.who.int/about/who-we-are.

ENDNOTES

INTRO

1   Barnhart (1960), 166.

CHAPTER 1

2   Encyclopedia Dubuque.

3   Scharnau.

CHAPTER 2

4   Library of Congress, The Germans in America. Chronology Guides.

5   Wende (1985), 95.

6   Boubil.

7   Wende (1985), 92.

8   Ibid, 92.

9   Ibid, 95.

10   Ibid, 97.

11   Ibid.

12   Ibid, 114.

13   Ibid.

14   Journey to America.

15   "History and Immigration. "History of German-American Relations 1683–1900."

16   Streeter Aldrich (1917).

17   Parker, *Iowa as It Is in 1855*, 18.

18   Treuer (2022).

19   Parker, *Iowa as It Is in 1855*, 66.

20   Ibid, 69.

21   Ibid, 74.

22   Ibid, 77.

23   Ibid, 74.

24   Ibid.

25   Ibid, 72–74.

26   Ibid, 143.

CHAPTER 3

27   Chin (2024).

28   Baxter and Nowrasteh (2021).

29   Streeter Aldrich (1959), 447.

30   "Bar. Affiliated with the Local History Network of the State Historical
     Society of Iowa and the Iowa Museum Association."

31   Street (2021).

32   German Americans' Contributions to Our Nation, Americans All.

33   Compendium News Staff.

34   History.com editorial staff, 2018.

35   German Immigration and Relocation in US History, Building a New
     Nation.

36   Tiggers and Shaffer (2000, p. 46).

37   Kwasky (1971).

38   Ibid, 94.

39   Ibid, 95.

40   DALZELL, Wilbur—Encyclopedia Dubuque.

41   Kwasky (1971), 61.

42   Dorchak (2008)

43   Kwasky (1971), 94.

44   Laurie (1994).

45   Gilbert and Adrian (2025).

46   US Department of Defense.

47   Encyclopaedia Britannica, (2023).

48   Weitz, Al, Letter to the Editor.

49   Ibid.

50   The Associated Press, 2022.

51   Justice Ruth Bader Ginsburg Offers Critique of Roe v. Wade During Law
     School Visit, University of Chicago Law School, (2022).

CHAPTER 4

52 Leopold (1975).

53 Ibid, 32.

54 Tiggers and Shaffer (2000), 32.

55 Dubuque, IA—Official Website | Official Website.

56 Ibid.

57 Kwasky (1971), 5.

58 Leopold (1975), 122.

59 Father Flanagan, Boys Town.

60 COMISKEY PARK—Encyclopedia Dubuque.

CHAPTER 5

61 Team (2024).

62 Hall (2019).

63 Ibid, 32.

64 Ibid, 37.

65 Pestritto, *The Birth of the Administrative State*.

CHAPTER 6

66 Kelly (2023).

67 Silverstein (2021).

68 Medication Abortion: Your Questions Answered, (2023).

69 Main Page—Ballotpedia.

70 Transforming Our World: The 2030 Agenda for Sustainable Development, Department of Economic and Social Affairs.

71 Merriam-Webster (2022) "Antisemitism," 52.

72 Ibid, 77.

73 Ibid, 169.

74 Schweizer (2024).

75 Ibid, 169.

76 Ibid, 185.

77 Council on Foreign Relations.

78 Defiance Publishing (2023).

79 How to Identify Critical Race Theory, the Heritage Foundation, n.d.

80 Merriam-Webster (2022), "Communism," 233.

81 Ibid, 246.

82 Reid, Scott A. (2025)

83 Creation Role and Purpose of Republican Government).

84 Merriam-Webster (2022).

85 Dictionary.com, Meanings & Definitions of English Words, (2025).

86 Merriam-Webster (2022), 307.

87 Ibid, 322.

88 Election Integrity, the Heritage Foundation.

89 The Electoral College, (2023).

90 Higley and John (2016).

91 The Corporate Governance Institute, (2023).

92 Dictionary.com, Meanings & Definitions of English Words.

93 Merriam-Webster (2022), "Fascism," 422.

94 The Fed Explained.

95 The Bill of Rights, 1789.

96 Ibid.

97 Merriam-Webster (2022), "Genocide," 486.

98 Beck and Haskins (2022).

99 Duignan and Brian (2025).

100 Merriam-Webster (2022), "Ideology," 575.

101 Ibid, "Indoctrination," 593.

102 Ibid, "Islamism," 621.

103 Merriam-Webster.

104 Merriam-Webster (2022), "Liberalism," 670.

105 Ibid, "Libertarianism," 670.

106 Merriam-Webster (2022) "Liberty" 670.

107 Ibid, "Maoism," 709.

108 Ibid, "Marxism," 709.

109 Wikipedia contributors, (2024).

110 Merriam-Webster (2022), "Nazism," 775.

111 Ibid, "Oligarchy," 810.

112 Ibid, "Patriotism," 852.

113 Ibid, "Progressivism," 942.

114 Ibid, "Propaganda," 935.

115 Ibid, "Racism," 962.

116 Ibid, "Revolution," 1003.

117 Ibid, "Socialism," 1014.

118 Technopolis.

119 Understanding Transgender People, Gender Identity, and Gender Expression, (2023).

120 Ostberg and René (2025).

121 Dictionary.com, Meanings & Definitions of English Words, (2025).

122 Merriam-Webster (2022), "Tyranny," 1279.

123 Merriam-Webster.

124 World Economic Forum.

125 World Health Organization.

CHAPTER 7

126 Merriam-Webster (2022), "Dissident," 336.

127 Gabbard (2024), 12–13.

128 Department of Justice, (2001).

129 White (1970), 170.

130 Franklin, Benjamin.

131 Stowe (1852).

132 *Harriet Beecher Stowe Meets Lincoln*, (1862).

133 Stowe (1852), 472.

134 Ibid, 477.

135 Reagan (1967).

136 Roth (2023), xl.

137 Merriam-Webster (2022), "Liberty," 670.

CHAPTER 8

138 Larson (2024), 42.

139 Cook (2024).

140 Ruane (2019).

141 Grant (2000), 57.

142 Ibid, 61.

143 Planned Parenthood's Reckoning with Margaret Sanger, (2021).

144 Ibid.

145 Grant (1993).

146 Ranji et al. (2025).

147 National Right to Life (2024).

148 Facts About Excessive Drinking, 2024.

149 Brenan (2025).

150 De Vise (2023).

151 Household Debt and Credit Report.

152 Streaks (2025).

153 Peterson Foundation, (2025).

154 The US Divorce Rate Has Hit a 50-Year Low.

155 McAllister (2025).

156 Branch (2025).

157 Tidwell, et al. (1991).

158 Riverboat Gambling—Encyclopedia Dubuque.

159 Topic: Sports Betting in the U.S., (2025).

160 American Gaming Association.

161 Bergman (2025).

162 Gaming and Gambling.

163 Orwell (1949).

164 Hankinson.

165 Batalova (2024).

166 Schweizer (2024).

167 How Prevalent Is Pornography?.

168 Ibid.

169 Men's Group.

CHAPTER 9

170 Declaration of Independence: A Transcription, (2024).

171 Spiro (2019).

172 Ibid, 8.

173 Dictionary.com, Meanings & Definitions of English Words, "Feudal"

174 *Dred Scott V. Sandford* [1857], (2024).

175 Spiro, 2019, 10.

176 Ibid, 10.

177 Milestones in the History of U.S. Foreign Relations—Office of the Historian.

178 Ibid.

179 Spiro (2019) 27.

180 US Government Agencies Involved in the Immigration Process, (2017).

181 About CBP)

182 Committee on the Judiciary and Subcommittee on Immigration Integrity, Security, and Enforcement (2024).

183 Narea (2024).

184 Ibid.

185 Ibid.

186 The New Colossus—Statue of Liberty National Monument (US National Park Service).

187 Ruiz Soto and Migration Policy Institute (2024).

188 Tanz, et al. (2024).

189 Schweizer (2024).

190 Startling Fact Sheet: Encounters of Chinese Nationals Surpass All Fiscal 2023 at the Southwest Border, (2024).

191 Wiegand, et al. (2016).

192 "Biden-Harris Administration Has Intentionally Left Us Vulnerable": Pfluger, Higgins Deliver Opening Statements in Hearing on Terror Threats From the Border—Committee on Homeland Security, (2024).

193 Geiger (2025).

194 Kitroeff, et al. (2023).

195 Ibid.

196 Asylum, USCIS, (2025),.

197 Temporary Protected Status: An Overview, (2025).

198 Ibid.

199 National Immigration Forum, (2021).

200 Kitroeff and Jordan (2023).

201 Ibid.

202 Ibid.

203 Oversight Committee Republicans Verified account, (2024).

204 Cohen (2020), 62.

205 Quiet Amnesty: How the Biden-Harris Administration Uses the Nation's Immigration Courts to Advance an Open-Borders Agenda, House Judiciary Committee Republicans, (2024).

206 Spiro (2019), 55.

207 USCIS, (2022).

208 Ibid, 29.

209 Hanson (2021) 121.

210 Ibid, 3.

211 ibid, p.1, Dr. Hanson quoting a speech from Mark Twain.

212 De Relaciones Exteriores.

213 Becoming a British Citizen.

214 Armenian Genocide (1915–1923).

215 Warfare 1914–1918 (Ottoman Empire/Middle East) / 1.0 / Handbook—1914-1918-Online (WW1) Encyclopedia, 2024).

216 Drpatwalsh (2016).

217 Ibid.

218 Othfors.

219 Captain (2013).

220 "Gul Djemal Lands Citizens."

CHAPTER 10

221

222 Lewis, C. S. (Zondervan: 2001) 120.

223 Karon (2002).